The
Market Segmentation
Workbook

Also Available for Readers

Exclusive Disk Offer

The charts in this workbook are intended for readers to fill in as they develop their own strategies for market segmentation. For those who would like to use the charts in a team situation, there is a simple disk available that allows readers to print exactly the same forms in A4 size. Ideal for team working, overhead projection, in-house training or for lectures, this gives the reader the opportunity to use the forms again and again.

The disk contains the following:

- the forms filled in as examples
- the forms blank and protected for printing
- simple instructions for printing these forms
- cross references to the book

The disk is available in $3\frac{1}{2}$ inch size. Price, including postage, packing and VAT, on application.

To order a copy please contact Customer Services, ITBP, Andover, Hants, SP10 5BE. Order telephone hotline: 01264 342923 quoting ref. no. 1861520115

Or for further information contact: Francesca Weaver on 0171 497 1422.

By the same authors,
Sally Dibb and Lyndon Simkin,
available from Routledge:

The Marketing Planning Workbook

The Marketing Casebook: Cases and Concepts

The Market Segmentation Workbook

Target Marketing for Marketing Managers

Sally Dibb and Lyndon Simkin

London and New York

First published 1996
by Routledge
11 New Fetter Lane, London EC4P 4EE

Simultaneously published in the USA and Canada
by Routledge
29 West 35th Street, New York, NY 10001

Typeset in Plantin Light by Solidus (Bristol) Limited
Printed and bound in Great Britain by Biddles Ltd, Guildford and King's Lynn

British Library Cataloguing in Publication Data
A catalogue record for this book is available from the British Library

Library of Congress Cataloging in Publication Data
A catalog record for this book has been requested

ISBN 0-415-11892-1

For Becky, Jamie and Abby

Contents

Figures and Charts

NB: Figures are for illustration, charts are for completion.

Figures

Charts

Preface

Market segmentation aims to

a) identify groups of customers with similar needs and purchasing behaviour, allocating them to market segments;

b) select which segments to target;

c) determine how to position products to appeal to the target markets; and

d) develop marketing programmes which convey the desired brand positioning.

Put in this manner, it seems simple. For most marketing managers – and many academics – market segmentation is far from straight-forward. This text aims to de-mystify the rigours of market segmentation: its workbook format presents clear guidelines and instructions for those wishing to re-examine their target markets.

The Market Segmentation Workbook aims to

- *be practical.* The ideas are actionable and structured in an easy-to-follow process.
- *offer step-by-step guidance.* Followed through, the stages outlined present a proven process of analysis, strategic thought and imple-mentable programmes.
- *provide thorough help.* Each stage is explained comprehensively.
- *result in workable recommendations.* The ideas and process are well tried and tested.
- *be academically rigorous while operationally viable.* The approach is founded on sound academic principles merged with business pragmatism.

The Market Segmentation Workbook is for

- Busy marketing managers who require direct guidance within a clear framework.
- Re-examining the marketplace: customer needs, target markets, competitive threats and general trends.

- Establishing marketing programmes which enhance customer satisfaction.
- Developing realistic, objective recommendations based on academically sound analyses.

The Market Segmentation Workbook is **not**:

- a detailed set of worked case histories, as applications to date are too confidential. The text does, though, contain numerous detailed illustrations.
- a marketing management text. There is, however, full explanation of incorporated theory and concepts, supported by extensive referencing.
- for marketing novices. Each step is carefully explained and illustrated, but practising marketing professionals will gain more from this book than managers from other functional areas or first-year undergraduates!

The Market Segmentation Workbook is logically structured:

- Introduction, overview of market segmentation, the ASP segmentation process: *Section I.*
- Essential marketing analyses for re-evaluating target markets: *Section II.*
- Strategic decision-making using the output from the analyses: *Section III.*
- Determining and controlling marketing programmes to implement the strategies: *Section IV.*

Progress is indicated in each chapter by way of the plan illustrated below. Each chapter has a checklist summarising the steps undertaken. It is *essential* that *The Market Segmentation Workbook*'s sections are tackled sequentially.

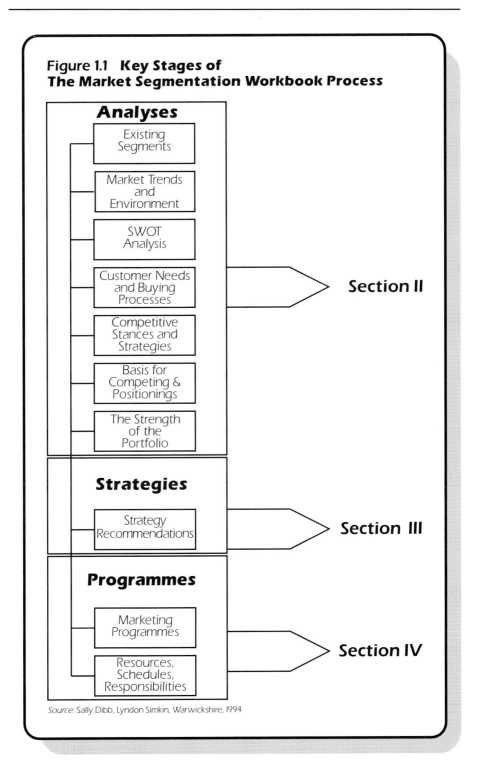

Figure 1.1 **Key Stages of The Market Segmentation Workbook Process**

Analyses
- Existing Segments
- Market Trends and Environment
- SWOT Analysis
- Customer Needs and Buying Processes
- Competitive Stances and Strategies
- Basis for Competing & Positionings
- The Strength of the Portfolio

→ **Section II**

Strategies
- Strategy Recommendations

→ **Section III**

Programmes
- Marketing Programmes
- Resources, Schedules, Responsibilities

→ **Section IV**

Source: Sally Dibb, Lyndon Simkin, Warwickshire, 1994

About the Authors

In 1991 Sally Dibb and Lyndon Simkin joined with US colleagues Bill Pride and O.C. Ferrell to produce *Marketing: Concepts and Strategies* (published by Houghton Mifflin). Now in its second edition, this text dominates the business school market in the UK, Eire, Benelux and much of Scandinavia. To coincide with the second edition of this text, Sally and Lyndon published *The Marketing Casebook: Cases and Concepts*, through Routledge in 1994. This innovative package created new ground by combining 15 real company cases with theory notes, glossary and readings to create a self-learn text.

Married with three children – Becky, James and baby Abby – Sally and Lyndon have been lecturing to MBAs and undergraduates at the University of Warwick Business School since the mid-1980s.

Sally has a BSc (management science) and MSc (industrial marketing) from UMIST in Manchester and a PhD (consumer marketing modelling) from Warwick. Lyndon was once an economic geographer (BA, Leicester) before switching to marketing (PhD) at the University of Bradford's Management Centre. Their current publications are in the areas of marketing modelling, market segmentation, marketing planning, marketing communications and services marketing. Consultancy is diverse, ranging from car parts, diggers, chemicals, cameras, IT to burgers; in the UK, Europe and beyond! Some of these experiences are touched upon in this text.

If you have any queries, please contact Sally and Lyndon by fax on 01926 851561 or by telephone at the University of Warwick on 01203 523523.

Readers finding the format of this workbook to their liking should note that a sister title is available, *The Marketing Planning Workbook*, London: Routledge, 1995.

Acknowledgements

We wish to thank several retail and services organisations whose personnel have assisted in the development of ideas utilised herein. In addition, we express our gratitude to four businesses: ICI, JCB, Zeneca and DRA. Without the co-operation of these companies this proforma would not have been possible. Specifically,

John Bradley, *JCB Corporate Marketing*
John Greaves, *Zeneca Fernhurst*
Sam Hay, *ICI Market Focus Bureau*
David A. Smith, *DRA CIS*

Jayne Ackroyd, *DRA*
Peter Corbett, *Dalgety Agriculture*
Tony Dinallo, *ICI France*
Ian Goodwin, *ICI Canada*
John Hall, *ICI USA*
Anita Hunt, *Tioxide UK*
Flavio Prezzi, *Zeneca Brazil*
Piet Smits, *Zeneca Fernhurst*
Lynne Stainthorpe, *Tioxide UK*
James Taylor, *Zeneca UK*
Luis Villa, *Zeneca Mexico*
Peter Whittle, *Tioxide UK*
Afranio Zardo, *Zeneca Panama*

Peter Jackson, *Adsearch London*
Robin Wensley, *University of Warwick Business School*

Section I

Scene Setting:
The Market Segmentation
Process

1

Introduction

Market segmentation is widely regarded to be one of the key elements of modern marketing. The technique is an analytical process which puts customers first, helps maximise resources and emphasises business strengths over competitors. Enthusiasts claim that this offers a route to more effective and better aimed marketing programmes, fewer direct confrontations with competitors and more satisfied customers. Not surprisingly, the popularity and acceptance of the approach has become increasingly widespread, transcending market, industry and national boundaries. However, while the benefits which segmentation offers are potentially great, the changes which are required may be difficult to apply in real business situations. The authors' experience across a range of market and industry situations demonstrates that practitioners must reconcile potential segmentation benefits with the realities of a well-entrenched company structure, distribution system and sales force. Such factors are rarely addressed in the academic and practitioner literature, leaving businesses alone to deal with the operational realities of moving forward from their existing view of the marketplace.

The segmentation process described in this book is founded on two fundamental beliefs: first, that the gap between academic research and the practical needs of marketing practitioners *can* be bridged and second, that putting market segmentation into practice need *not* be a protracted and awkward process. Segmentation is, after all, firmly based on the principles of marketing analysis, which are widely understood across all industries. The key to successful segmentation seems to lie in developing a series of easy to follow stages, which are accessible to marketing practitioners and which take realistic account of the existing practical constraints imposed by the marketplace and the way in which the business currently operates.

1.1 Customers May Share Needs

The underlying premise of market segmentation is that not all customers have the same product or service needs. For this reason it is rarely appropriate to use a single sales and marketing programme to attract all potential customers. True mass marketing, it seems, is at an end and companies must respect the variety of needs which customers display and reflect this in their marketplace offerings. Equally, with a few exceptions, it is unrealistic for companies to customise their marketing programmes for individual customers. Market segmentation allows a balance to be struck between the heterogeneity of customers on one side and the limited resources of suppliers on the other. This is achieved because customers sharing broadly the same product/brand requirements and buying behaviour can be grouped together to form a *market segment*. Customers within a market segment will tend to have homogeneous consumption patterns and product attitudes which are different from those in other segments.

Most companies acknowledge the existence of segments of customers with similar needs and market more than one product in order to appeal to more than one group of customers. Many successful companies attribute their success to identifying and meeting the needs of certain kinds of customers. Few companies have the resources to offer different products to all customer segments in a particular market. Instead, they concentrate on the most lucrative or beneficial segments.

This is market segmentation: the identification of sub-groups of customers who share common needs; the selection of which of these groups or segments to target; and, the presentation to these targeted customers of well defined sales and marketing programmes emphasising a distinctive product image or brand positioning.

1.2 Undertaking a Market Segmentation Evaluation

Businesses which carry out a review of their segmentation strategy, may do so either as a stand-alone study, or as part of a business or marketing planning exercise. Organisations beginning the process generally do so with considerable optimism. This is not particularly surprising as the research and analysis involved in the evaluation will inevitably identify new ways of grouping customers who share similar needs. These needs continually evolve and change, being affected by general trends in the marketplace, a company's product offerings and those of competitors, as well as the views of fellow customers. A re-evaluation of market segments will usually bring benefits: better product orientation and understanding of customers' exact needs, plus insights into the development of a sustainable competitive advantage.

Unfortunately, the optimism which is characteristic of the start of the process may have ebbed away by the time the segmentation project reaches its conclusion. Diagnosis of potential difficulties is essential if the process is to be effectively implemented. So what are the potential problems? Companies initially may be confused about the purpose of the exercise and may not fully appreciate the likely outcomes. Second, the segmentation process – the steps which must be taken to identify a new scheme of segments – may not be understood. Finally, many businesses are simply unsure of where to begin their analysis. Providing that these difficulties are recognised and dealt with positively, businesses should be able to enjoy the benefits which segmentation offers. The segmentation process described in this book involves a step-by-step approach which is specifically designed to overcome such problems.

1.3 Sympathy with Existing Marketing Arrangements

Underlying market segmentation there is a need for realism. Most businesses already have loyal customers, entrenched distribution channels and well established sales and marketing initiatives. Market segmentation is often seen as signalling change, yet long standing distribution arrangements and marketing programmes cannot be revised overnight. Alterations to the product portfolio or key customer targets cannot happen without thought for the consequences. Indeed, radical change may be undesirable, wasteful and counter-productive in the short term and perhaps difficult because of contractual obligations with distributors and customers. Ultimately the market segmentation evaluation is only worth incorporating into revised marketing strategies if there are clear financial, competitive and market benefits. Furthermore, these benefits must be seen to outweigh the practical and financial costs associated with implementing the change. However, businesses must avoid adopting a short-term view, particularly as the market segmentation benefits may require longer term investment. Research has shown that UK businesses are often more concerned about short term profits than longer-term growth and survival. Appropriate application of market segmentation can help to make the necessary investment in the future of a business.

Strategic marketing texts frequently overlook the realities of implementing segmentation and apparently assume that businesses have total control over all elements of their operating environment and are able, at will, to sweep away existing structures and begin afresh. The authors' consultancy and research experience across a wide range of industries shows clearly that this is not the case. Businesses may be severely limited in an operational sense when re-evaluating their segmentation approach.

This book begins by acknowledging the types of practical constraints which businesses face and which can inhibit the implementation of market segmentation, and then it attempts to operate from within these constraints. The segmentation process which is described starts with an objective assessment of the business's current delineation of target markets and then moves forward in a series of carefully linked stages to review and progress the segmentation in a manageable, market-orientated manner.

1.4 The Analysis, Strategy and Programmes for Implementation Segmentation Process

The segmentation approach described in this book is based on the principle that successful marketing strategy requires three clear, distinct, yet related stages, each tackled thoroughly, objectively and in a logical sequence: Analysis, Strategy and Programmes for Implementation. Put simply this involves the gathering of marketing intelligence, followed by strategic thinking, then the development of sales and marketing programmes to facilitate implementation of the identified target market strategies. In more detail, the ASP segmentation approach proposed involves three basic stages:

1 *Analysis.* Information collection for the segmentation exercise. This involves the analysis of the existing customer base and business performance plus core analyses of customers, market trends, competition, brand positionings, company situation and the strengths of the product portfolio.

2 *Strategy.* Carrying out segmentation, targeting and positioning. Turning the enhanced understanding of the marketplace into strategic decisions and the targeting of appropriate customer groups. This targeting should emphasise any differential advantages and adopt a suitable positioning within the target segment(s).

3 *Programmes for implementation.* The development of marketing programmes which implement the segmentation strategy. The determination of mechanisms to control the implementation of these programmes.

Experience suggests that when followed through, this segmentation programme results in a wide range of tangible benefits:

- A fresh look at core markets. Outdated information and opinions are reviewed.
- Improved understanding of customer needs and buying behaviour. The background analyses demand a full review of basic customer requirements, buying processes and product attitudes.
- Maximised use of company strengths and appropriate use of resources. The analysis of assets and resources allows the business to determine the most appropriate future direction.
- A more market-focused business leading to increased customer and distributor satisfaction.
- Identification of segment and target market priorities. Carrying out the core analyses allows the appropriate strategy decisions to be made.
- Full utilisation of competitive edges. Matching company strengths/assets with customer needs allows the potential advantages to be identified and exploited.
- Development of more appropriate marketing programmes. Enhanced understanding of the company strengths, market trends, customer needs and competitive positionings results in more finely tuned marketing programmes.
- A sense of direction and understanding across the business together with enhanced internal communication between and within functions. Making the segmentation process work requires different parts of the business to co-ordinate activities, resulting in a number of side benefits.

The structure of this book has been carefully determined to ensure that each step in the segmentation programme is presented in a logical sequence. The reader should therefore attend to each section in turn.

- *Section I* (Chapters 1 and 2) provides a review of the market segmentation process giving an important backdrop to the programme presented. The section ends by considering each of the **Analysis, Strategy** and **Programmes for implementation** elements of the segmentation process.
- *Section II* (Chapters A1–A7) examines each of the core analyses which form the basis for any determination of segments, target markets and related marketing programmes. An overview and instructions are given for each of the following analyses: existing sectors/segments; market trends and the marketing environment;

SWOT analysis; customer needs, expectations and buying processes; competition and competitors' strategies; bases for competing and brand positionings, and the product/segment portfolio.

- *Section III* (Chapter S1) discusses how to turn the findings and implications from the analyses into strategic decisions: how best to group customers into segments; which groups – or market segments – the company should target to maximise its competitive position and use of resources; how to position brands and products in the marketplace.
- To be of any benefit to the business under examination, these strategies will inevitably require modifications to be made to the existing sales and marketing programmes. The final stage in the segmentation process is to review the necessary programmes, resources, responsibilities and scheduling for implementation of the segmentation strategy, and to establish control procedures. These issues are highlighted in *Section IV* (Chapters P1 and P2).

Finally, it is important to stress that this book is not intended as a marketing management text book. When worked through, section by section, the material will allow the user rigorously to update his/her business's marketing intelligence and marketing analyses. The user will then be led into well founded strategic decisions and encouraged to ensure that the target market strategy is actioned through detailed, realistic marketing programmes. The flow chart illustrated in Figure 1.1, which will be referred to throughout the subsequent sections to illustrate the interrelation of chapters and the reader's progress, summarises the rationale of this book. (Subsequent appearances of this figure will carry the title 'Checklist of Progress'.)

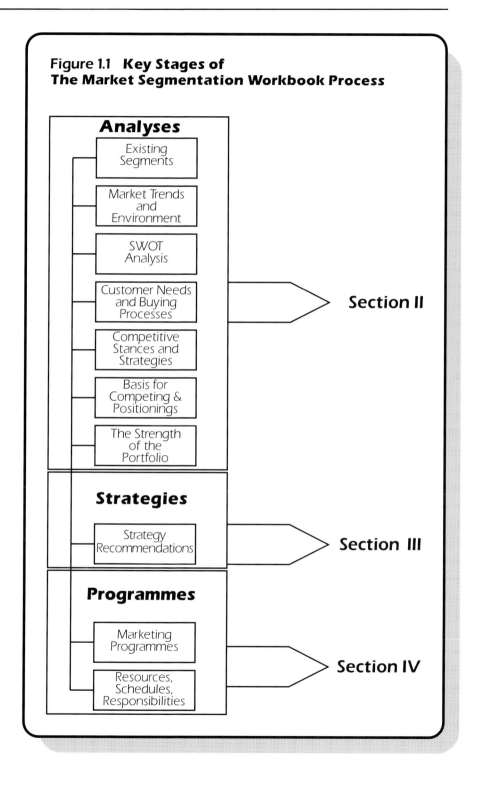

Figure 1.1 Key Stages of The Market Segmentation Workbook Process

Analyses
- Existing Segments
- Market Trends and Environment
- SWOT Analysis
- Customer Needs and Buying Processes
- Competitive Stances and Strategies
- Basis for Competing & Positionings
- The Strength of the Portfolio

→ **Section II**

Strategies
- Strategy Recommendations

→ **Section III**

Programmes
- Marketing Programmes
- Resources, Schedules, Responsibilities

→ **Section IV**

2

The Segmentation Process

2.1 Introduction

Having a detailed understanding of the varying needs and requirements of different customers is fundamental to the principles of marketing. Although companies may recognise the breadth of such needs it is usually unrealistic to customise products to suit each individual. Moving away from mass marketing towards a market segmentation approach, where the focus is on a particular group (or groups) of customers, is an increasingly popular way of dealing with diverse customer needs.

Many companies believe that marketing success is linked to how effectively their customer base is segmented. This is because market segmentation helps companies to satisfy diverse customer needs while maintaining certain scale economies. The process begins by grouping together customers with similar requirements and buying characteristics. Next, the organisation can select the group(s) on which to target its sales and marketing. A marketing programme can then be designed to cater for the specific requirements and characteristics of the targeted group(s) or segment(s) of customers. This marketing programme will aim to position the product or service directly at the targeted consumers. Such positioning will take into consideration the offerings of competing organisations within the same segment.

The benefits that a market segmentation approach offers are many and varied. These benefits include a better understanding of customer needs and wants, which can lead to more carefully tuned and effective marketing programmes; greater insight into the competitive situation, which assists in the identification and maintenance of a differential advantage, and more effective resource allocation. Rarely is it realistic to target 100 per cent of a market, so focusing on certain segments allows organisations to make efficient use of their resources.

2.2 Using Market Segmentation

The benefits offered by market segmentation can help companies take advantage of marketing opportunities which might otherwise be missed. These opportunities can be related to activities in new or existing product markets:

- *Market penetration* allows companies to increase their percentage of sales in existing markets by taking sales from competitors. For example, this can be achieved by an aggressive and well targeted promotional campaign. A soft drinks manufacturer may seek to extend sales of diet drinks through a combined advertising and sales promotion drive.
- *Product development* involves offering new or improved products to current markets, through the expansion of the product range. Washing powder manufacturers have sought to capitalise on consumers' concerns about the environment with the launch of so-called environmentally friendly products aimed specifically at this segment.
- *Market development* involves the sale of existing products to new markets, typically by finding new applications. For example, the makers of Evian mineral water developed a new use for the product by packaging it in an atomiser and selling it as a skin moisturiser.
- *Diversification* is about seeking opportunities in new markets, by offering new products. The innovativeness of 3M company has allowed the business to diversify into a wide range of markets.

2.3 The Segmentation Process

Any market segmentation programme consists of three distinct stages. It is important to understand these stages fully before making any major decisions about how different markets should be segmented. The illustration below demonstrates the relationship between the key stages which are explained further in subsequent sections.

Put simply, the underlying principle of the three stages is that 'similar' customers can be grouped. For example, an audience of 100 managers asked about their favourite car model might have given 100 different responses. However, some of those asked required the benefits offered by sports cars, others those of 4-wheel drive off-road vehicles, while a further group's needs could be satisfied by executive cars. In situations where such 'similar' consumers can be collected into large enough groups, there is obvious potential for companies wishing to target such *segments*.

Sub-sections 2.4, 2.5 and 2.6 of this chapter review the segmentation process in more detail.

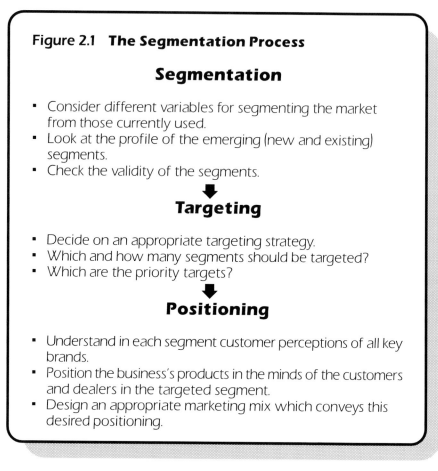

Figure 2.1 **The Segmentation Process**

Segmentation

- Consider different variables for segmenting the market from those currently used.
- Look at the profile of the emerging (new and existing) segments.
- Check the validity of the segments.

Targeting

- Decide on an appropriate targeting strategy.
- Which and how many segments should be targeted?
- Which are the priority targets?

Positioning

- Understand in each segment customer perceptions of all key brands.
- Position the business's products in the minds of the customers and dealers in the targeted segment.
- Design an appropriate marketing mix which conveys this desired positioning.

2.4 Carrying Out Segmentation

2.4.1 The Key Steps

Carrying out segmentation, the stage where customers are aggregated into groups, involves two basic steps:

Step i

Segmentation variables (also called *base variables*) are used to group together customers who demonstrate similar product requirements and buying behaviour. When choosing appropriate segmentation bases it is necessary to select those which clearly distinguish between different product requirements. For example, some customers of freezer ready-meals may be concerned about their weight and fitness. These customers may seek a different range of products than consumers without such concerns.

Figure 2.2 illustrates different segmentation bases which can be used in consumer markets. Many of the same segmentation bases also apply in industrial or business-to-business markets. Probably the most popular industrial or business-to-business segmentation bases include geographic location, type of organisation, trade category, customer size/characteristics, product usage and business sector.

Either a single base variable or several in combination can be applied. For example, a common approach is to link geographic territory with customers' industrial sector, such as with Mexican maize farmers or German food bottlers.

It is important to be aware that choosing segmentation bases is a fairly subjective process, so it is rarely possible to assert categorically that there is *one* best way to segment a particular market. Different organisations may view the market and how it is segmented in different ways. What matters is that there are clear-cut benefits resulting from the chosen scheme.

Step ii

Once segments have been identified using one or a combination of the base variables above, as much as possible must be done to understand the characteristics of the customers in those segments. This understanding will make it easier for the marketer to design a marketing programme which will appeal to the segment targeted. Building up a fuller picture of the segments is called *profiling* and uses *descriptor variables*. Descriptors can include variables relating to customer characteristics or product related behavioural variables. In fact, the more extensive the picture, the better.

Sometimes people find the distinction between *base* and *descriptor variables* confusing. Just remember that *base* variables are used first to allocate customers to segments, whereas *descriptors* help later in building up a profile of segment membership.

Figure 2.2 Segmentation Bases in Consumer Markets

Basic Customer Characteristics

Owing to the ease with which such information can be obtained, the use of these variables is widespread.

- **Demographics**

  Age   Sex

  Family   Marital Status

  Race   Religion

  Family Life-Cycle

- **Socio-Economics**

  Income   Occupation

  Education   Social Class

- **Geographic Location**

  Country   Region

  Type of Urban Area   Type of Housing

  Urban/Rural

- **Personality, Motives and Lifestyle**

  Consumer's Personality

  Motives for Purchasing/Consuming

  Consumer's Lifestyle and Aspirations

Product-Related Behavioural Characteristics

- **Purchase Behaviour**

  Brand Loyalty versus Triggers for Switching

- **Purchase Occasion**

  Novelty   Frequency

  Event   Dealer Location

- **Benefits Sought**

  Perhaps the most popular consumer segmentation base: the benefits sought by the consumer from purchasing, consuming, having the product or service

- **Consumption Behaviour and User Status**

  Heavy users versus light and non-users

- **Attitude to Product/Service**

  Different Consumers' Perceptions

2.4.2 Essential Qualities for Effective Segments

As has been stated, there is no single way to segment a market, but there are some criteria which can help to decide on the robustness of a particular approach. Before implementing a segmentation scheme it is helpful to check that the segments satisfy the following conditions by being:

- *Measurable*: it must be possible to delimit, measure and assess the segments for market potential. Remember that excessive demand can be as difficult to handle as no demand at all!
- *Substantial*: in order to warrant marketing activity, the identified segment must be large enough to be viable and therefore worthwhile targeting with products/services.
- *Accessible*: having identified a market segment, and checked its potential viability, the marketer must be able to action a marketing programme with a finely developed marketing mix for targeted customers. Sometimes the similarities between customers within a particular segment are insufficient to implement full marketing programmes.
- *Stable*: there must be an assessment of a segment's short, medium and long-term viability, particularly in the light of competitor and marketing environment changes. Segments rarely remain the same over time, so it is necessary to weigh up the extent and impact of likely changes.

The importance of satisfying these segment criteria is clearly illustrated by research from the automotive aftermarket. In this market replacement vehicle parts are sold to end-customers by installers (perhaps a national chain of outlets or a vehicle manufacturer's agent). These parts are then installed in the end-customer's vehicle. A study designed to segment these installers successfully identified and validated appropriate groupings. However, attempts to profile the segment members were dogged with problems. The result was that the identified segments were not sufficiently accessible.

2.5 Targeting

Once segments have been identified, decisions about how many and which customer groups to target must be made. The options include:

- *Mass marketing strategy*: offering one product concept to most of the market, across many market segments. Although scale economies can be achieved, there is the risk that few customers will be adequately satisfied.

- *Single segment strategy*: concentrating on a single segment with one product concept. This is relatively cheap in resources, but very risky if the segment should fail.
- *Multi-segment strategy*: targeting a different product concept at each of a number of segments. Although this approach can spread the risk of being over-committed in one area, it can be extremely resource hungry.

Which target segment strategy a company adopts will depend on a number of market, product and competitive factors. Each of these must be carefully considered before a decision is made about segments to be targeted. Before making a commitment to any segment it is essential to consider the following issues:

- *Existing market share/market homogeneity.* How similar is the market to current areas of activity and does the company have market share or brand awareness in related areas on which it can build?
- *Product homogeneity.* Does the company have relevant expertise on which to build in a related product field? Does the make-up of the overall product portfolio dictate direction?
- *Nature of competitive environment.* What is the level of competition in the market and how is this changing over time? How will entering the segment affect the competitive status quo?
- *Market trends and the marketing environment.* Where do the numbers (market sizes, etc.) lead? Are there any marketing environment issues likely to help or hinder particular market segment growth and viability?
- *Customer needs.* How extreme/easy to satisfy are customer requirements?
- *Segment size, structure and future potential.* How big is the segment, how is it made up and how is it likely to develop in the future?
- *Company resources.* Does the company have the resources to target the segment under consideration? Are there strengths and weaknesses which relate to target prioritisation?

Taking a balanced view of these factors helps companies make decisions about the viability of particular segments and ensures that resources are appropriately targeted. For example, a children's wear retailer which traditionally sold clothing for the under eights, decided not to enter the eight- to ten-year-old market because of aggressive competition and limited company resources.

2.6 Positioning

Once segments have been identified and targeting decisions made, it is necessary to consider exactly how and where the product – and marketing programme – is to be positioned within the target segment(s). *Product positioning* centres on the decisions and activities used to create and maintain a firm's product concept in the customers' minds. Such activities must reflect the positions occupied by competing companies and products within the market. *Market positioning* is arranging for a product to occupy a clear, distinctive and desirable place – relative to competing products – in the minds of target customers.

Positioning forms a direct link between the target market strategy and the marketing programmes. The positioning is determined so as to effectively appeal specifically to targeted customer needs. The marketing programmes have to facilitate this communication.

The desired position vis-à-vis competitors' brands is partly dictated by the existing position: large shifts of perception are often unrealistic, costly and take time. It was a decade before certain car manufacturers lost their reputation for rust or unreliability in the 1970s. Equally, not every brand wants to be pitched at the 'top end' of a market: Lada and Yugo have carved out useful market positions, without being at the quality/expensive extreme in their marketplace.

2.6.1 Perceptions in Customers' Minds

Successful positioning involves ensuring the product is perceived by the target customers to satisfy their desires and expectations. The position of the product therefore relates to the attributes which those customers ascribe to it, such as its standing, its quality, the value it delivers, its price, the type of people who use it, its strengths and weaknesses, and any other unusual and memorable characteristics it may possess.

The whole of the marketing mix is important in developing an effective positioning. Product attributes, price points and distribution channels all have a role to play, but promotional activity is probably the most fundamental element because it provides the mechanism through which the positioning is communicated to the target audience.

2.6.2 Steps in Determining a Positioning Plan

The following steps describe the route to achieving a particular product positioning. This process can be applied to new products requiring positioning for the first time, or to the repositioning of existing products.

1. Define the segments in a particular market.

2. Decide which segment(s) to target.

3. Understand what the target customers expect and believe to be most important when deciding on a purchase.

4. Develop a product or brand which caters specifically for these needs and expectations.

5. Evaluate the positioning and images, as perceived by the target customers, of competing products/brands in the selected market segment(s).

6. Using the characteristics of a product/brand, the needs and expectations of target customers, and their perception of competing brands' positioning, select an image which sets the product or brand apart from the competing brands – ensuring the chosen image matches the aspirations of the target customers. The selected positioning and imagery must be credible.

7. The marketer must communicate with the targeted customers about the product – the promotional element of the marketing mix – as well as making the product readily available at the right price, with the associated development of the full marketing mix.

8. Try to be as realistic as possible. If repositioning, remember that major shifts in perceptions take time and resources and are not always possible. Customers and distributors have long memories!

2.6.3 Perceptual Maps

Perceptual mapping is an approach which many companies use to understand customer perceptions of different products/brands in the marketplace. The technique is based on a variety of mathematical approaches designed to describe the customer perceptions on one or a series of 'spatial maps'. The result is a visual picture of the perceptions, showing the relative positionings of different products, brands or companies – for example, Figure 2.3. The dimensions selected for the mapping should preferably have been identified through customer research. Confirmatory research can then be used to identify the relative positionings of the products, brands or companies to be plotted.

Positioning maps such as the one shown in Figure 2.3 can help marketers to develop more realistic and effective marketing pro- grammes. They can also provide valuable assistance in exercises to reposition a particular product or brand. However, to achieve huge moves on a perceptual map requires tremendous resources – and often much patience – as customer perceptions take time to shift. Major brands Coca-Cola and McDonald's have images which have been built over an extensive time period. In general, effective repositioning takes considerable time and resource, and major switches in attitudes to the product or brand cannot usually be achieved without re-branding or new product ranges.

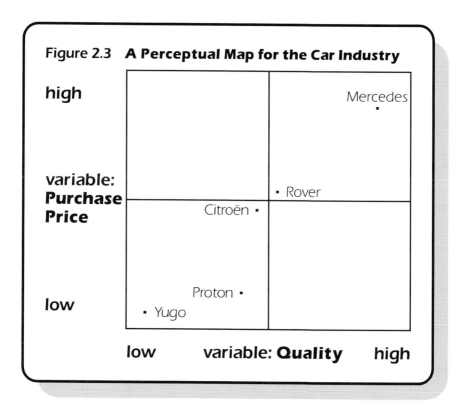

Figure 2.3 A Perceptual Map for the Car Industry

2.7 The Practicalities of Market Segmentation

2.7.1 Implementation Difficulties

Despite the obvious benefits which market segmentation offers, attempts to impose new or altered segmentation schemes frequently encounter practical problems. Although a particular scheme may pinpoint key customer groups more precisely, existing organisational and distribution structures may present implementation difficulties. Research evidence from a wide range of industries suggests *implementability* is a key criterion in successful segmentation exercises. Ultimately, revised target market strategies must be actioned through revised sales and marketing programmes. Radical changes, however, particularly to distribution may not be feasible or cost effective. Even in such instances, though, minor modifications and improvements will be possible.

2.7.2 Selecting Segmentation Bases

In order to reconcile some of these practical difficulties, it is helpful to focus on how the base variables for the segmentation part of the process are determined. This is important because it will directly impact on the degree of change required by a new segmentation approach.

There are different schools of thought relating to the selection of segmentation base variables. These are referred to as the unordered, two-step and multi-step approaches.

- *Unordered base selection.* Little advice is offered regarding the selection of base variables. Instead the emphasis is on the managerial usefulness of the resulting segments.
- *Two-step approaches.* The underlying assumption is that different variables can be weighted according to their importance in the segmentation. In this sense there is a simple hierarchical basis to the approach. Perhaps the most well known is the Macro Micro model proposed by Wind and Cardoza (1974). The first step, the macro stage, involves the use of general organisational factors such as company demographics, geographic location or product usage. Often this relates to the company's existing approach to grouping customers, so is minimally disruptive. The micro stage will only be undertaken when insufficient insight is given from the macro stage. This second stage involves the identification of sub-segments (micro segments) within the macro groupings. The variable used at this stage is related to characteristics of the decision making unit.

- *Multi-step approaches.* The nested approach, proposed by Bonoma and Shapiro (1983), is a development of the two-step models. Here there are different levels of variables through which the marketer must progress. The outer levels of the nest consist of easier to measure and more general variables, such as demographics and operating factors. The inner levels comprise harder to measure, more personal variables, such as situational factors and personal characteristics of individuals in the decision-making unit.

There are a number of positive and negative aspects to each school of thought. Unordered approaches can be unsystematic and result in too broad a view of the market. A further difficulty is that more complex segmentation using a number of interacting base variables is not properly catered for. Although the Macro Micro model allows for more flexibility in the choice of segmentation bases, the micro segments are only considered within the broad macro segments. This is also inflexible because interaction between members of the macro segments is not allowed. The multi-step approach gets around these difficulties by recognising that segmentation may rely on the inter-actions between a combination of different types of variables.

The segmentation process described in this book attempts to capitalise on the pragmatism offered by the multi-step approach and the conceptual simplicity of the two-step method. The underlying principle is of minimal disruption, so that the business begins its segmentation review with a consideration of its existing segmentation approach. Following a systematic process of market analysis, micro or sub-segments can then be identified within these broad groupings. This second step is then followed by a remixing of sub-segments, using appropriate new and existing base variables, until a more appropriate solution is found. Figure 2.4 illustrates the approach.*

*Some users of this book may wonder how complex multivariate analysis, such as cluster analysis or multi-dimensional scaling, fits within the segmentation approach which has been described. Although it is beyond the scope of this book to explore this area, practitioners with this type of statistical expertise may wish to use it to analyse available data at any of the stages described in Figure 2.4. Some useful references are given below to support such activities. Those without such heady expertise should find the more pragmatic approach described in this book to be well within their grasp.

Aldenderfer, M.S. and Blashfield, R.K. (1984) *Cluster Analysis*, Beverly Hills: Sage.
Alt, M. (1990) *Exploring Hyperspace: A Non-Mathematical Explanation of Multivariate Analysis*, Maidenhead: McGraw-Hill.
Everitt, B.S. (1993) *Cluster Analysis*, London: Arnold.
Lilien, G.L. and Kotler, P. (1983) *Marketing Decision Making: A Model-Building*

Figure 2.4 The Steps of Segmentation

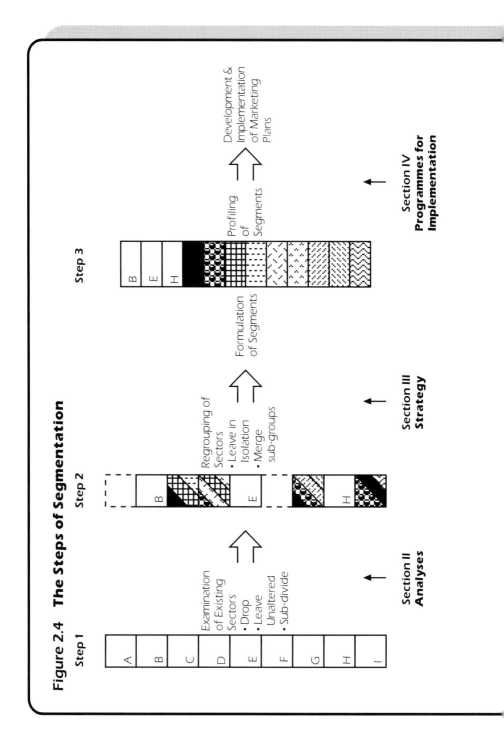

Step 1

| A |
| B |
| C |
| D |
| E |
| F |
| G |
| H |
| I |

Examination
of Existing
Sectors
- Drop
- Leave
  Unaltered
- Sub-divide

Step 2

B

E

H

Regrouping of
Sectors
- Leave in
  Isolation
- Merge
  sub-groups

Step 3

B

E

H

Formulation
of Segments

Profiling
of
Segments

Development &
Implementation
of Marketing
Plans

Section II
Analyses

Section III
Strategy

Section IV
Programmes for
Implementation

Explanation

At Step 1 the business lists its existing breakdown of customer groups. Typically these will be based on product groups, customer type, industrial sector, geographic territory in industrial markets, or perhaps location, social class, behaviour, brand loyalty in consumer markets. The groupings may be based on a couple of these dimensions.

An evaluation of these groupings in terms of key customer values (KCVs) and buying behaviour may result in some sectors being dropped, left as already defined/grouped or further sub-divided/grouped into additional sub-groups.

Example

In the example, at Step 1, this business revealed it used a classification giving 9 customer groupings. Research suggested in Section II of this book revealed this classification was flawed when examining KCVs and buying behaviour. In other words, the existing groups of customers did not demonstrate homogeneous needs and buying processes. These groupings needed revising.

Step 2 reflects the initial revisions/modifications to the original customer groupings. After some groupings may have been dropped, left alone or further sub-divided. Step 2 results in a new and probably more lengthy list of redefined sectors or customer groupings.

An evaluation across this list of new groupings in terms of KCVs and buying behaviour will reveal certain similarities between a few combinations of sub-groupings.

By Step 2, the original classifications of 9 customer groups is revised. Two of the original 9 no longer exist (these customers having all been reallocated). Three of the original 9 remain unaltered, being robust homogeneous groups of customers. Four of the original 9 are further subdivided into 14 groups of 9 different classes of customers in terms of KCVs and buying behaviour.

The three unaltered groupings are B, E and H.
The new sub-groupings are:

■ *with three occurrences:*

▨ *with three occurrences:*

▦ *with two occurrences:*

For Step 3, there will be a further revised listing of customer groupings as sub-groups sharing similar KCVs and buying behaviour are joined together to form homogeneous customer segments. Each segment will have a unique profile

Once the final list of segments has been determined, the business must identify which segments it wants as target priorities. For each target market, a marketing plan must outline detailed programmes for implementation.

By Step 3, the unaltered remaining three original customer groups are joined by 9 new segments. These 9 new segments are the 14 new sub-groups merged with their similar neighbours to form segments each containing customers with similar needs and buying behaviour.

each with one occurrence:

Typically, businesses which have followed this prescribed approach have developed segmentation programmes which progress on two levels:

a) the broad macro segments have constructively been sub-divided into more homogeneous sub-groups of 'similar' customers, permitting more carefully tuned sales and marketing activities; and

b) some newly identified sub-segments have been re-grouped across the former divides to form new, more homogeneous customer segments.

Through the segmentation process proposed, any target market changes required are the result of objective and thorough marketing analyses: change is never just for the sake of change. Even if no modifications to strategy seem necessary, this segmentation process leads to an enhanced understanding of market trends, customers' needs, competitors' strategies and any competitive edge for the business: marketing programmes can maximise opportunities. The process is also therefore a useful aid to marketing planning.

2.8 Summary

This chapter has reviewed the theoretical background to market segmentation. The benefits and uses of the approach have been explored and the three stages of market segmentation reviewed. These stages comprise segmentation, targeting and positioning. When carrying out the first stage managers must consider the base variables being used to allocate customers to groups and identify appropriate descriptors. Segments which are identified must be measurable, substantial, accessible and relatively stable. At the targeting stage of the process, possible options include a mass marketing, single segment or multi-segment strategy. Positioning involves creating and maintaining the firm's product concept in the customers' minds. The chapter ends by reviewing the practicalities of market segmentation and implementation difficulties. Different approaches are reviewed for selecting segment bases and a model proposed for minimally disruptive segmentation. This model forms the basis for the segmentation process described in this book.

Approach, New York: Harper and Row.
Tabachnick, B.G. and Fidell, L.S. (1983) *Using Multivariate Statistics*, New York: Harper and Row.

Section II

Core Analyses

Before strategic decisions can be made regarding the allocation of customers to segments or the selection of the business's target segments, there are certain background marketing analyses which must be conducted.

The inclusion of objective and thorough marketing analyses are vital. The segmentation process can bring significant benefits to the company and renewed vigour in its market, but these must not depend on the subjective assumptions of managers alone. The views in the analyses must also be those of the marketplace, particularly of dealers and customers.

The central analyses follow a logical sequence and support the analysis/strategy/programme (ASP) market segmentation process described in the introduction. Each analysis is important and helps to complete the understanding of the market and to give a sound level of marketing intelligence on which to base decisions.

By the end of this section you will have carried out the following analyses:

- A review of the existing customer base; history of existing segments and their worth to the company.
- Market trends and the marketing environment.
- Company strengths, weaknesses, opportunities and threats (SWOT) in respect of customer needs, market trends, competitive activity and internal company capabilities.
- Customer needs and expectations, now and in the near future. Customers' buying processes and influencing issues. Direct customers and end-users.
- Competition and competitors' strategies.
- Basis for competing and brand positionings in the marketplace.
- The balance and strengths of the business's product portfolio.

Section II Contents

Analyses 1

Existing Segments/Sectors

A1.1 Introduction

An understanding of customers is at the heart of any segmentation exercise. Most organisations' existing customer bases reflect the needs and wants which those companies have proved able to satisfy. Having a clear view of the customer base, over time, helps companies determine where future opportunities may lie. Understanding the requirements of current customer groups/segments is vital if companies are to satisfy the core customer base. However, it is also necessary to appreciate the contribution made by key customer groups and individual accounts. This helps determine a sensible allocation of resources.

The existing view of customer segments and primary sales targets will be based on a mix of historical information about the market and individual customers and managerial insight. Some, but not all, of this information will probably be valid, up-to-date and useful. The company's systems and structures, particularly in the context of distribution coverage, sales priorities and the sales force, may be well thought through and organised. However, in most organisations, 'historical perceptions' of which customers/markets are important tend to cloud judgement on current customer targeting and sales forecasting. Similarly, the basis on which customers are currently grouped into 'segments' may have been logical. However, with customer needs and behaviour changing all the time, and with competition and market trends creating ever evolving marketplaces, there is, for any organisation, always a need to re-examine the importance of individual customers, customer groupings and targets.

By the end of this chapter you will have summarised, described and listed the key customer values (KCVs) for your company's existing customer groups/segments. The relative importance of these segments historically will have been determined and an explanation given for major changes over time. Finally, ABC Sales/Contribution charts will have been completed for all market segments and key customer accounts.

A1.2 Examining the Existing Customer Base

There are five key stages to re-examining the existing customer base, priorities and segments. These stages create a background analysis which illustrates the degree of 're-segmentation' required, and the strengths from the existing approach which must be incorporated within any recommended changes to strategies:

(i) State how customers are broken down currently into sub-groups or segments by the business's managers. For example, by customers' industry sector; their customer type; their purchasing patterns (seasonal, regular, etc); the types of products purchased from the business; territory, or whatever. Are such categorisations commonplace within the industry?

One company had customer groups based on country and crops grown by its customers. A separate organisation used geographic territory and its own product groups as customer grouping criteria. A third business grouped customers subject to their buying loyalty and frequency of order. Most businesses have their own mix of criteria, but product group, customer type and geography are popular dimensions. What does your business use?

In markets where there are only a few, large customers, each customer may be currently treated as a segment. If this is so, consider initially individual customers.

(ii) For each existing segment or identified group of customers, summarise *their* product, dealer/distribution, sales and marketing needs which the business must aim to satisfy. In other words, the Key Customer Values (KCVs) – the principal sales, product and marketing aspects valued or demanded by customers. Ideally, this type of information should come from customer research.

In one industrial segment, KCVs were just-in-time delivery, product customisation, credit terms and international distribution by suppliers. In a consumer segment, KCVs were identified as range width, availability, technical expertise of sales personnel, and country of origin.

(iii) With the understanding of customers used in addressing steps i and ii, describe the current segmentation *descriptors* on which existing strategies hinge. For example, industrial sector; geographical territory; heavy or light users; technically aware or technically retarded customers; brand loyals or price orientated, etc. There may well be a mix, such as a customer segment described as 'heavy users, brand

Chart A1.1 **Summary of Existing Market Segments/Sectors**

NB: Example is based on the shampoo Market

Customer Group or Segment	These Customers' Key Needs (KCVs)	Adopted Descriptions Used by Company to Describe Segment
1 *Combined shampoo and softener brigade*	– *Convenience* – *Price* – *Brand*	*'2 in 1s'*
2 *Babies*	– *Brand reputation* – *Re-assurance* – *Convenience* – *Value*	*Babies and Big Softies*
3		
4		
5		
6		
7		
8		

Actions:
- Rank segments in column 1 in order of current importance to company.
- For each segment, rank the Key Customer Values listed in column 2.
- Define KCV term if required so as to avoid ambiguity.

loyals, northern French pig farmers'; or 'price conscious, national supermarket chains'; or 'Yuppie car buyers', etc.

Steps (i) to (iii) are summarised in Chart A1.1. Note that the contents of Chart A1.1 are used as the input to various subsequent

Chart A1.2 Historic Importance of Segments

Rank Order of Segments by Year										
Segment	t-9	t-8	t-7	t-6	t-5	t-4	t-3	t-2	t-1	Current year (t)
1										
2										
3										
4										
5										
6										
7										
8										

Reasons for Major Changes

Actions:
- Rank each segment's importance to the business over the years. The business may view sales volumes, market share, profitability or contribution as a measure of importance.
- Explain any big moves/rank changes.

charts, so must be considered carefully.

(iv) It is likely that the composition of the segments in Chart A1.1 has changed over time, and that the importance of each segment to the company has altered. Tabulate for the past ten years the rank order of importance of these segments, adding explanatory footnotes where the running order alters significantly (for example, if a segment ranked second five years ago is only currently ranked ninth; perhaps because of changing technology in production, revised customer tastes or economic recession). Importance could be in terms of sales volumes, market share, profitability or contribution. See Chart A1.2.

(v) Summarising these year on year moves should have sent a few alarm bells ringing. Why is so much importance placed on segment 'X'? Why is the sales force still devoting so much resource to segment 'Y'? What about segment 'A' – suddenly it seems more important. Is it?

The final stage in examining the recent history of the segmentation, and for assessing the current view of segments, is to evaluate the financial worth of these segments – and of major individual customers – to the business. The most common approach is to examine sales and contribution – the financial value to the company – in an ABC Sales: Contribution (Pareto) Analysis.

A1.3 The ABC Sales: Contribution (Pareto) Analysis

A1.3.1 Market Segments

This analysis can be conducted at either Product or Product Mix level. The aim is to show the number of sales and contribution to the business. This analysis helps companies to identify the relative value of different market segments/customer accounts and assists the allocation of resources. An example of an ABC Sales: Contribution chart is shown in Figure A1.1.

(i) *Data*. List out, segment by segment, current sales in either volume or turnover. Turnover (for example in £s or $s) is more common.

List out, segment by segment, current levels of financial contribution (sales revenue minus all variable costs).

(ii) *Graph*. On a standard, two dimensional (X-axis and Y-axis) graph, plot out sales and contributions. Depending on data ranges, it may be necessary to use log scales:

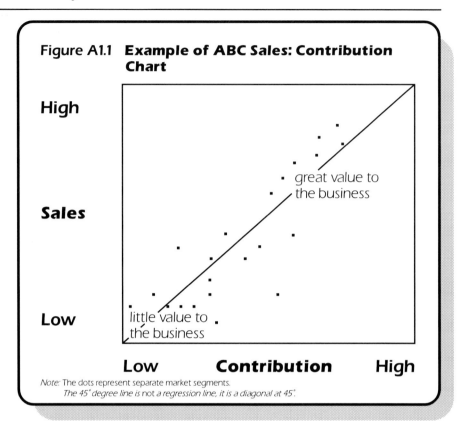

Figure A1.1 **Example of ABC Sales: Contribution Chart**

High

Sales

great value to
the business

Low

little value to
the business

Low   **Contribution**   High

Note: The dots represent separate market segments.
The 45° degree line is not a regression line, it is a diagonal at 45°.

- Y-axis (vertical): sales;
- X-axis (horizontal): contribution.

To scale the axes' highest ranges required, sum up (a) sales and (b) contributions. These totals give the high points on the graph.

(iii) *Evaluation.* In an ideal world, the dots on the graph – each dot represents a segment – would be located at the top right of the graph: high sales and high contribution. Or, 'sell a lot, make a lot', 'A' class segments. Typically, however, this is not the case. The majority of segments fall at the bottom left of the graph (low sales and low contribution: 'C' class segments), or they have reasonably high sales, but low contributions ('B' class).

(iv) *Diagnosis.* Not all of the plotted segments will be close to the 45 degree diagonal line optimum (from bottom left to top right of the ABC chart). There will be outliers requiring attention.

    A question mark should hang over any segment located in the bottom left of the graph: these segments are draining sales and marketing resources, without offering any obvious return to the company. Is there any benefit in continuing to service these segments? Is a presence needed to protect the business's other products and segments from competitive inroads? Would other customers worry if the business pulled away from these low-benefit customers? Are there seasonal reasons for this currently poor return? If the answers are 'no', new targets may be required.

Can improvements be made? High volume segments to the upper left of the 45 degree line, with low contributions, would be of tremendous value if contributions were increased by only a few per cent.

Similarly, high contribution segments where currently volumes are low (those plotted to the lower right of the 45 degree line) are crucial targets: even a minor increase in sales volumes should be very lucrative to the company.

Clearly such 'movements' and improvements are not always possible. For segments in the bottom left of the graph, harsh decisions may be required, as these markets seem to be of little value to the company.

Chart A1.3 can be used to summarise the results of the ABC analysis at the segment and individual customer account levels.

When a leading European car manufacturer conducted this analysis, out of 44 countries into which its models were exported, only two showed a significant contribution, one of which also managed high sales volumes. Two other countries achieved high sales volumes, but with no positive contribution. When the analysis was extended into each segment, country by country, only 12 segments out of nearly 150 in the 44 countries were financially worth while targeting as export markets. Others had potential, but there was a significant 'tail' which had evolved historically and required urgent surgery. The car manufacturer in question is now neither independent nor European-owned.

A1.3.2 Individual Customer Accounts

So far this ABC Sales: Contribution analysis has concentrated on the segment level. The completed analysis should help to identify which segments have the most value for the business. Segments which contribute relatively little can also be identified. The second level of analysis is to examine individual key customer accounts in a similar manner.

This analysis can be either by Product or Product Mix.

(i) *Data.* List out, customer by customer, current sales in either volume or turnover. Turnover (e.g.: £s or $s) is more common.

List out, customer by customer, current levels of financial contribution (sales revenues minus all variable costs).

(ii) *Graph*. On a standard, two dimensional (X-axis and Y-axis) graph, plot out sales and contributions:
- Y-axis (vertical): sales;
- X-axis (horizontal): contribution.

(iii) *Evaluation* and (iv) *Diagnosis*. The final two stages, evaluation and diagnosis, are the same as the approach for assessing whole segments. The ease of dropping customers of little value – those in the bottom left of the graph – should be greater, as should the need to lose such customers.

Chart A1.3   ABC Sales: Contribution Chart

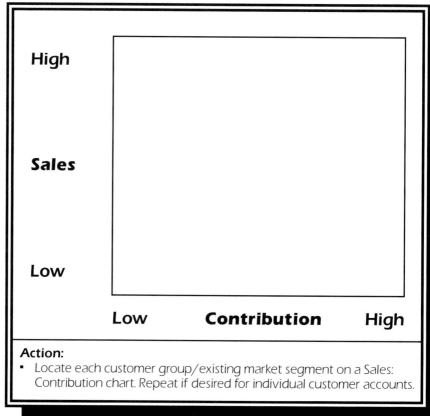

Action:
- Locate each customer group/existing market segment on a Sales: Contribution chart. Repeat if desired for individual customer accounts.

A1.4 Summary

These straightforward analyses have presented an important overview of the nature of existing customer groups or market segments, their key characteristics, their relative importance in recent years to the business, and their current value in terms of sales volume and contribution.

These analyses may demonstrate a need to re-think segmentation and to keep abreast of a changing marketplace. If the examination of current segments has not prompted modifications to target market strategy and marketing programmes, the outcome from the analyses described in the remainder of the Analyses section probably will encourage changes. There will, though, be significant strengths in the existing approach to segmentation and customer targeting, and therefore to sales and marketing. These background analyses, plus some analyses detailed in the following pages, will highlight these strengths and help to ensure that this review of market segmentation builds upon the company's existing view of its marketplace and incorporates all the most relevant, up-to-date and vital information.

By the end of this chapter you will have summarised, described and listed the key customer values (KCVs) for your company's *existing* customer groups/segments. The relative importance of these segments historically will have been determined and an explanation given for major changes over time. Finally, ABC Sales: Contribution charts will have been completed for all market segments and perhaps for key customer accounts.

A1 Checklist: Existing Segments/Sectors

Please read and complete the following checklist.

1. What you should have found out:

Before moving on to the next chapter you should have a clear understanding of how your company's customers are currently grouped, the variables which are used to group them and you should be able to describe typical characteristics of segment members. You should also have summarised the requirements (KCVs) of these customer groups and built an impression of the relative importance of these segments, to your business, over the last ten years. ABC sales/contribution charts should have been completed for all market segments and key customer accounts, giving an understanding of the financial worth each provides.

If you have not yet collected the necessary information to achieve this, it is vital that you return to this chapter as soon as possible. It will not be possible to thoroughly work through this workbook without this background information.

2. Charts which should have been completed:

Make a record of your progress by completing the following charts:

	Status of Analysis		
	Complete	Partly filled	Not complete
A1.1: Summary of existing market segments	❑	❑	❑
A1.2: Importance of current segments, last 10 years	❑	❑	❑
A1.3: ABC sales: contribution chart	❑	❑	❑

Be prepared to revisit these charts if/when further relevant information becomes available.

3. Information collected:

The following areas of information are relevant to this chapter. Please indicate your progress in collecting this and other relevant information:

	Information		
	Collected	Collection under way	Not collected
Variables used to group customers	❑	❑	❑
Segment by segment key customer values	❑	❑	❑
Segment by segment descriptions	❑	❑	❑
Segment by segment current sales volume	❑	❑	❑
Segment by segment current sales turnover	❑	❑	❑
Segment by segment financial contribution	❑	❑	❑
Customer by customer current sales volume	❑	❑	❑
Customer by customer current sales turnover	❑	❑	❑
Customer by customer financial contribution	❑	❑	❑
Other.	❑	❑	❑

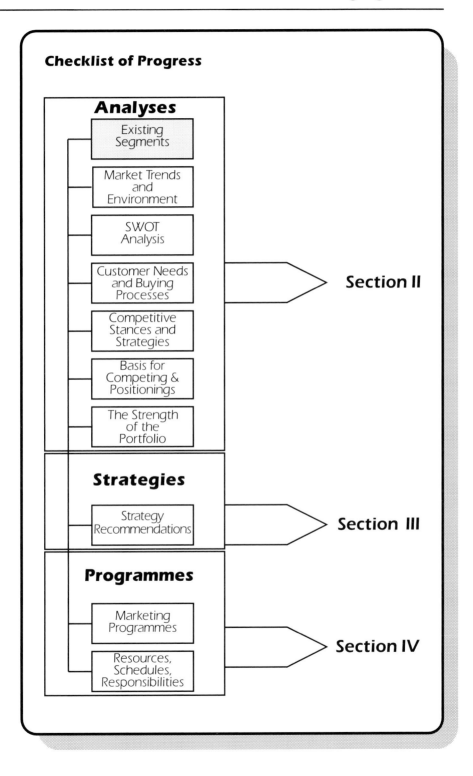

Analyses 2

Market Trends and the Marketing Environment

A2.1 Introduction

Any programme of market segmentation requires an informed understanding of prevailing trends in the relevant market. This is vital in assessing which segments are likely to give the best future rewards and for making targeting decisions. An appreciation of market trends allows organisations to target segments with high sales volume and value, while avoiding those which are in decline. Numerical market trends information must be backed up with an understanding of the impact of the marketing environment upon the business. The marketing environment has been defined as 'those external forces that directly or indirectly influence an organisation's acquisitions of inputs and generation of outputs' (Dibb *et al.* 1994). The different aspects of the marketing environment elements are described below. The relevance of each of these elements will vary for different markets.

By the end of this chapter you will have summarised recent core market trends and made predictions for the next five years. These trends will cover sales volume, sales value, market size, market share, customer base and number of principal dealers and distributors. You will also have examined those elements of the marketing environment which impact upon your business.

A2.2 The Trends in the Market

A2.2.1 Market Trends

Being aware of trends in the market helps identify opportunities and pinpoint areas where resources should be focused. This is particularly important when making targeting decisions. The following market trends should be monitored closely:

- Sales: volume size
- Sales: financial values
- Market size
- Market shares
- Numbers and sizes of customers
- Numbers, sizes and geographic coverage of dealers/retailers

A2.2.2 Recording the Trends in the Market

Core market trends can be summarised numerically. Using Chart A2.1, record the current and historical values for the trends listed. If appropriate, additional columns for other relevant information can be added. Predicting likely future trends in these areas, although never entirely accurate, can help identify future opportunities. Using the historical data and market knowledge as a starting point, predict likely future figures for these trends. These predictions can be refined as further information becomes available.

Chart A2.1 Core Market Trends and Predictions

Year	Market Name	Sales Volumes (Units)	Sales (£s/$s)	Profit-ability (£s/$s)	Market Size	The Business's Market Share	Number of Principal Customer	Number of Principal Dealers/ Distributors
t-5								
t-4								
t-3								
t-2								
t-1								
Current year (t)	UK pigment, bulk	22 tonnes	£6.2 m	£0.45m	88 tonnes	25%	55	3
t+1								
t+2								
t+3								
t+4								

Actions:
- Complete as many columns as possible. Sales and market share are essential.
- Information beyond the current year should be based on forecasts/estimates.
- Principal customers: most businesses have an '80:20' split - the bulk of business (e.g. '80%') comes from a minority of customers (e.g. '20%') - see ABC analysis in Chart A1.3.

A2.3 The Marketing Environment

A2.3.1 The External Trading Environment

The marketing environment comprises aspects of the trading environment over which the company has very little direct control, but which can tangibly affect the way in which the company does business and performs.

For example, until recently car manufacturers could dictate to their franchised car showrooms that only certain models be displayed, that rival manufacturers' vehicles could not be sold alongside their own models, and that the franchisee could not build another manufacturer's showroom on the same site. Changing EC regulations will remove such controls from manufacturers, and showrooms will eventually be allowed to sell several manufacturers' cars under one roof. The manufacturers have had little control over this change of policy, but will need to react quickly with dealer initiatives to keep franchisees loyal.

Some organisations may already have a reasonable level of understanding about the marketing environment. However, often such information is not circulated to those company personnel requiring it. This analysis makes sure that the key trends are identified, then information is collected, shared and incorporated within marketing strategy development.

To monitor changes in the marketing environment, marketers must undertake regular scanning and analysis. *Environmental Scanning* is the process of tracking information from observation, secondary sources (particularly the trade press and government reports) and marketing research. Many companies have individual marketing managers or committees whose function is to collect and collate data related to trends in the market and aspects of the marketing environment. Experience with companies from a range of industries suggests that allocating the monitoring task for aspects of the marketing environment to certain individuals or groups is a useful way of sharing the workload. Regular update meetings can help ensure that the collected information is shared.

The marketing environment generally is broken into two key areas, termed the *macro* marketing environment and the *micro* marketing environment. Information on all aspects of these two areas provides vital scene-setting for the segmentation programme.

A2.3.2 Macro Environment

The main elements of the macro environment are legal, regulatory, political, societal, technological and economic forces. The impact of each of these elements will differ according to market and geographic area. Where more than one market and/or geographic area is being considered, it is necessary to consider the relevant environmental aspects for each.

Legal forces

Many laws influence marketing activities; for example: pro-competitive legislation and consumer protection legislation.

Regulatory forces

Interpretation of laws is important, but so is an understanding of the enforcement by the various governmental and non-governmental regulatory bodies; for example: government ministries, local authorities, trade and professional associations.

Political forces

Many marketers view the actions of government as beyond influence, while others successfully lobby and influence the policy making and legislating bodies of central and local governments. It is important to realise that the lobbying of other organisations can affect your company, so taking control of this area is important.

Societal forces (culture)

These are the dynamics and workings of society: groups and individuals often ignore the activities of companies and marketers until they impinge – usually negatively – on their lifestyles and choices. Perhaps the most significant example currently is consumer pressure on companies to produce products which are less harmful to the earth's environment, with less waste, and which are produced in a more ecologically sensitive manner: the 'greening consumer'.

Technological forces

These refer to the technological expertise with which to accomplish tasks and goals. Technology is quickly evolving and changing, affecting how people satisfy their needs and lead their lives. It also affects what products marketers can bring to the marketplace, and how they are presented to customers.

Economic conditions

General economic conditions – recession or boom – will impact on any market, as will customer demand and spending behaviour. These are important considerations for any marketer, particularly as such conditions are prone to dramatic changes, patterns and fashions.

A2.3.3 Micro Environment

The elements of the micro marketing environment are aspects which are peculiar to the individual company/organisation concerned – rather than market specific. The control which the company has over these factors is variable. The key items of the micro environment are direct and substitute competition, supplier influence/power, company's resource base and the buying power of customers.

Competition: direct, substitute and new

It is necessary to consider the nature and degree of competition in a product area from similar products. In addition, whether there is a possibility of competition from substitute products. The stability of the competitive situation and likelihood of new entrants are also relevant.

Supplier influence/power

Companies usually prefer independence and often seek the opportunity to exert control over their suppliers. Control is not always possible: suppliers, particularly in situations where there are very few or if the products supplied are innovative or unique, can become uncomfortably strong. Co-operation can reduce the risks posed by such suppliers, so it is important to understand these relationships and the role of influence and power within them. The stability of the relationships is also an important issue.

The company's resource base

The resource base in terms of supplies and materials, finance, people, time and goodwill is generally in the control of the business itself. There are occasions, though, when trends in the marketplace and in the marketing environment act to strengthen or weaken the resource base. For example new industry-wide working practices; legislation; altered banking policies; customer pressures and demands, all alter the resource base. Activities which can affect the availability of resources must be monitored.

Customers' buying power

Customers' requirements and perceptions must constantly be monitored (see chapter A4), but it is possible for underlying trends in the market to result in increased or decreased customer buying power. The result of either change will have significant impact on the business's performance and the likelihood of such changes in buying power must be checked.

No matter what the organisation or market, there are always elements of the marketing environment which directly impact on the competence of a company's performance. This means that the segmentation process must include an analysis of the relevant elements of the marketing environment for each market under consideration.

A2.3.4 Recording the Key Marketing Environment Issues

The importance of different aspects of the macro or micro marketing environment will vary for different companies and markets. Care should be taken when eliminating aspects of the marketing environment from the analysis. It is too easy to ignore a particular issue simply because it has not been relevant in the past.

Often managers think about market trends and developments which may affect their company's business, but they fail to articulate these concerns. In a market segmentation programme, they must be discussed, as market trends will inevitably impact on the choice of which segments to target, and perhaps on how products and brands should be positioned in the marketplace.

Marketing environment trends need to be recorded (see Chart A2.2). This table is a simple summary so that key issues are brought to the attention of senior managers. Inevitably, where different teams are dealing with different parts of the business, common themes will emerge. This should force the business to prioritise these areas and allocate managers or teams to monitor and evaluate separate topics. As has already been indicated, allocating resources in this way can help reduce individuals' workloads, aid communication and maintain momentum.

Chart A2.2 The Marketing Environment Issues

E.g.: based on the European airline industry

Summary of Core Issues

Macro Environment

(legal, regulatory and political, societal, technological, economic)

EC competitive legislation/Gov. de-regulation
Safety concerns
Civil conflicts (wars)
Economic recession
Customer comfort desires
CNAA regulations

Micro Environment

(direct and substitute competition, new entrants, supplier influence, customer buying power)

Channel Tunnel
Price competition from channel ferries

Principal Implications for the Business of These Issues

Must strive to match customer needs
Lobbying of regulators
Need to assess Channel Tunnel's impact
Consider more routes/nodes

Actions:
- Consider the wide range of potentially relevant concerns.
- Be prudent and objective – list only important concerns.
- List the most important issues first.
- Have evidence to support these assertions.

A2.4 Summary

The analyses carried out in this chapter have enabled you to summarise a number of important marketing trends including sales volume/value, market size/share, number and size of customers and number and geographical coverage of dealers. During this chapter you have also considered aspects of the marketing environment which are likely to impact upon your business now and in the future.

These types of analyses are important for a number of reasons. Firstly, by understanding and monitoring the market trends, your business is more likely to be able to predict potential growth areas and identify strategic opportunities. The wider marketing environment: legal, regulatory, political, societal, technological, economic forces will also have a significant impact on your business's future opportunities, as will the micro environment: competition, supplier influence and power, company's resource base and customer buying power. It is inevitable that some of these aspects will impact upon and constrain your business's actions. For example, the level of direct competition in a particular segment may make it unattractive to you. Having a thorough understanding of the most significant areas of impact is vital if your business is to take appropriate actions/decisions. This chapter provides a first look at some of these areas. Customers, their needs, wants and buying behaviour and competition are reviewed in more detail in subsequent analysis chapters.

A2 Checklist: Market Trends/The Marketing Environment

Please read and complete the following checklist.

1. What you should have found out:

Before moving on to the next chapter you should have an understanding of current and historical market trends. You should also have made predictions about likely future trends in the same areas. In addition, you should have recorded information about relevant aspects of the marketing environment. If you are operating in more than one market, you will need to fill in copies of the relevant forms for each.

If you have not yet collected the necessary information to achieve this analysis, it is vital that you return to this chapter as soon as possible, and certainly prior to considering future targeting priorities.

2. Charts which should have been completed:

Make a record of your progress in completing the following charts:

	Status of Analysis		
	Complete	Partly filled	Not complete
A2.1: Core market trends and predictions	❏	❏	❏
A2.2: Summary of core marketing environment issues	❏	❏	❏

Be prepared to revisit these charts if/when further relevant information becomes available.

3. Information collected:

The following areas of information are relevant to this chapter. Please indicate your progress in collecting this and other relevant information:

	Information		
	Collected	Collection under way	Not collected
Sales volume	❏	❏	❏
Sales value	❏	❏	❏
Market size	❏	❏	❏
Profitability	❏	❏	❏
Company market share	❏	❏	❏
Size of principal customer base	❏	❏	❏
Number of principal dealers/distributors	❏	❏	❏
Other.	❏	❏	❏
Legal forces	❏	❏	❏
Regulatory forces	❏	❏	❏
Political forces	❏	❏	❏
Societal (cultural) forces	❏	❏	❏
Technological forces	❏	❏	❏
Economic conditions	❏	❏	❏
Competition	❏	❏	❏
Supplier influence/power	❏	❏	❏
Company resource base	❏	❏	❏
Customer buying power	❏	❏	❏
Other.	❏	❏	❏

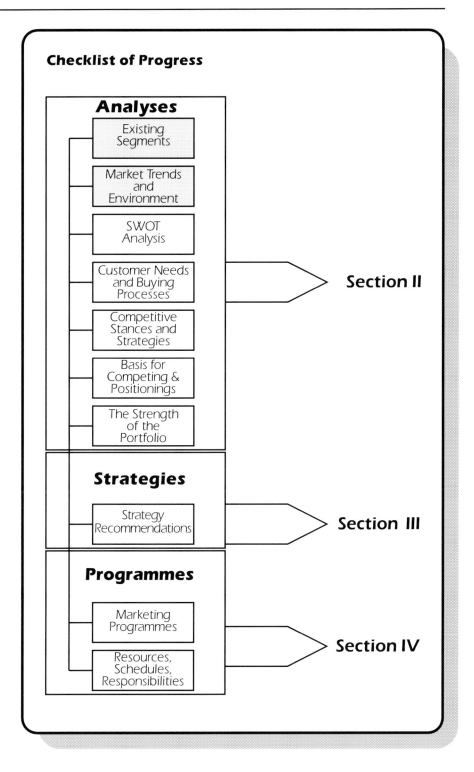

Checklist of Progress

Analyses

- Existing Segments
- Market Trends and Environment
- SWOT Analysis
- Customer Needs and Buying Processes → **Section II**
- Competitive Stances and Strategies
- Basis for Competing & Positionings
- The Strength of the Portfolio

Strategies

- Strategy Recommendations → **Section III**

Programmes

- Marketing Programmes
- Resources, Schedules, Responsibilities → **Section IV**

Analyses 3

SWOT Analysis: Strengths, Weaknesses, Opportunities and Threats

A3.1 Introduction

Any segmentation analysis must begin with a broad understanding of the market situation in which a business operates and an appreciation of the types of opportunities and threats which might be faced. The *SWOT* analysis, one of the most commonly implemented analyses in marketing, provides an excellent starting point for this type of review. Put simply the SWOT helps to identify and structure a business's **s**trengths, **w**eaknesses as well as the available **o**pportunities and **t**hreats. This is achieved because the SWOT forces managers to consider the match between internal strengths and weaknesses and market opportunities. The quality of the match helps to determine in which broad areas the organisation should develop its business and eventually directs allocation of resources among segments.

This chapter considers the strengths, weaknesses, opportunities and threats for the segments or markets under review. A range of inputs should be used to determine the relative importance of each SWOT issue listed. By the end of this chapter you will have developed a full SWOT grid for each segment or market. The points listed under each heading (e.g. strength) will be ranked in order of importance: the number one strength will appear first.

A3.2 Developing Robust SWOT Analyses

A simple format for presenting the SWOT is illustrated in Figure A3.1: strengths, weaknesses, opportunities and threats. The conceptual simplicity of the SWOT has made it both accessible to managers and vulnerable to misuse. On the positive side, understanding of how to use the SWOT is widespread. Managers need neither extensive databases nor formal training. Almost anyone with a smattering of company and market knowledge can develop a simple SWOT. On the downside, the technique's inbuilt simplicity can lead to analyses which are hurried and relatively meaningless, containing issues as vague and ambiguous as 'product performance', 'modern facilities', 'prices'. Additionally, users may forget the need to be objective and rely on outdated or unreliable information.

Figure A3.1 **The SWOT Grid**

Internal	**Strengths**	**Weaknesses**
	Internal issues which are directly relevant to the customers under consideration. These issues must be narrow in focus.	
External	**Opportunities**	**Threats**
	External issues relating to a range of environmental areas such as legal/ political/regulatory/societal/economic/ technological and economic.	

Following a number of basic rules can help avoid misuse and maximise the robustness of the SWOT analysis:

Rule 1: Carefully define the scope of each particular SWOT. Companies frequently develop generic analyses to cover the entire business. These may well be too general to be particularly useful to managers considering the opportunities in particular markets or segments. Narrowing the SWOT to focus on a particular segment, for example, ensures that only the key strengths, weaknesses, opportunities and threats are considered.

Rule 2: Understand the distinction between the SWOT elements: strengths, weaknesses, opportunities and threats. Strengths and weaknesses are issues internal to a company and are therefore under its control. Opportunities and threats relate to aspects of the marketing environment and are not therefore under the control of the organisation.

Rule 3: Strengths and weaknesses can only be viewed as such if this is how they are perceived by the customers. It is necessary only to include the most pertinent strengths and weaknesses. Remember these strengths and weaknesses must have been defined in the context of competitors' offers. A strength is only a strength if it is seen as such by the marketplace. For example, product quality is only a strength if the performance is strong relative to competing products. Finally, endless lists of issues detract from those which are key. For this reason, strengths and weaknesses should be ranked to show their importance *in the customers' eyes*.

Rule 4: Be objective and use a broad base of inputs to generate the issues for the SWOT analysis. It may not always be possible to base the analysis on extensive marketing research, However, SWOT grids developed by only one individual are rarely as accurate or offer as much insight as those which come from group discussion and sharing of ideas. It is important that the SWOT is not merely a collection of managers' hunches. As far as possible the SWOT must be based on objective facts and on marketing research findings.

Rule 5: Avoid wide-ranging and ambiguous statements. All too often a SWOT grid is weakened by the inclusion of sweeping general statements, which would probably be meaningless to most customers. The more finely-tuned the issues included, the more useful the SWOT is likely to be. Figure A3.2 provides a useful illustration of this point. For example, **modern facilities**, listed as a strength would, for most customers, be an ill-defined and meaningless issue. However, this issue might usefully be broken down into a number of more relevant strengths and weaknesses from the customer's viewpoint:

modern facilities . . .	Strengths:	motivated staff
		evidence of investment
		image of success
	Weaknesses:	capital tied up
		hefty loan repayments.

Many of the issues listed in Figure A3.2 can be analysed in this way. Some of the sub-issues will be relevant to customers, others will not. The key is to include only those which the customer and the marketplace would perceive as important.

Figure A3.2 Example of a Poor SWOT Analysis

Strengths	Weaknesses
Experience Facilities Staff Expertise Impartiality Product Range Product Performance	Product Age Knowledge of Customers Prices Resources
Opportunities	**Threats**
Market Growth Legislation Internal Market Customer Needs Eastern Europe Struggling Competitors Government Support	Foreign Markets EC Subsidies Street Works Act Substitute Technologies

Note: This SWOT is poor because the issues seem jumbled; the points are too broad and ambiguously defined; many issues are internal views and take no account of the marketplace's views.

A3.3 Internal Environment Issues: Strengths/Weaknesses

A range of internal issues can be included in the strengths and weaknesses boxes. The following categories of information are typical of the areas which may be incorporated. Each SWOT will be different and may include one, a few, or all of the following issues. Each issue may appear in the strength or the weakness box, depending on customer perceptions:

- *Marketing.*
  Product
  Pricing
  Promotion
  Marketing Information/Intelligence
  Service/People
  Distribution/Distributors
  Branding and Positioning

- *Engineering and new product development.* As the relationship between engineering and marketing grows, these aspects will become increasingly important. For example, close links between new product development teams and the marketing department may allow feedback from customers to feed more directly into the product design process.
- *Operations.*
  Production/Engineering
  Sales and Marketing
  Processing orders/Transactions
- *People.*
  R&D
  Distributors
  Marketing
  Sales
  After Sales/Service
  Processing/Customer Service
  Their skills; wages/benefits; training and development; motivation; conditions; turnover. These are aspects central to the successful implementation of the customer focused marketing philosophy and the marketing strategy.
- *Management.* Sensitive and often contentious, but sometimes management structures and philosophies need altering to facilitate the successful implementation of a marketing strategy; such issues should be raised.
- *Company resources.* These resources will directly impact on the availability of finance and people and will therefore affect the ability of the business to take advantage of particular opportunities.

A3.4 External Environment Issues: Opportunities/Threats

The threats and opportunities are outside the control of the business. In this sense they are external issues which relate strongly to the marketing environment elements. The environmental analysis conducted earlier and discussed in Analysis 2 may offer a useful starting point for this part of the SWOT. The core features to consider include:

- *Legal/Regulatory/Political.* The actions of governments in terms of their handling of policy, as well as the legal and regulatory requirements with which companies must abide.

- *Societal forces (Culture).* These forces directly affect business when unhappy consumers bring pressure on organisations which are perceived to be acting in an unacceptable manner.
- *Technological.* The technological skills which help a business to meet its objectives affect the products which consumers are offered and their reactions to them.
- *Economic conditions.* The effects of general economic conditions which shape customer demand and spending behaviour.
- *Competition.* The nature and scale of the competitive threat. A range of issues warrant consideration:
    Intensity of rivalry
    Threat of entry
    Market's customer needs
    Bargaining power of buyers, distributors, suppliers
    Ability
    Pressure from substitutes

A3.5 Recording the SWOT Analysis

For each segment or market under review, list the most important (of most concern/likely influence on the business) issues in each of the four elements of the SWOT grid – Strengths, Weaknesses, Opportunities and Threats. See Chart A3.1. In each of the four sections of the SWOT, ensure that the points listed are in ranked order of importance: put the number one threat first, and so on. Make the SWOT as focused as possible: for example, if necessary develop a new SWOT analysis for each market segment or customer group. There is no point listing numerous issues: emphasise only those points of most impact on the business. Be objective: can the assertions be backed up with evidence (quotations, letters, trade statistics, press reports, government publications, dealer feedback, customer comments)? Make sure that the analysis is customer-orientated, rather than being too inwardly focused. Each time an issue is listed it can help to pose the following questions:

- Are we sure that this is true?
- How sure are we?
- How do we know?
- Is this likely to change soon?
- Is this point relevant/important/meaningful to our customers?
- Have we considered the position relative to our competition?

Chart A3.1 **The SWOT Analysis**

Strengths	Weaknesses

Opportunities	Threats

Actions:
- Rank (list) points in order of importance.
- Only include key points/issues.
- Have evidence to support these points.
- Strengths and Weaknesses should be relative to main competitors.
- Strengths and Weaknesses are *internal* issues.
- Opportunities and Threats are *external*, marketing environment issues.

What are the core implications from these issues?

Managers often produce SWOT grids for each leading competitor and for separate markets, revealing a company's relative strengths and weaknesses and ability to face the identified threats and opportunities. This is a useful exercise in identifying the attractiveness of the opportunities available and in weighing up the business's ability to pursue them.

A3.6 Summary

This chapter has reviewed the development of a SWOT analysis for each market or segment under consideration. This simple approach allows companies to review the opportunities present in the marketplace and weigh up their capabilities for pursuing them. An appreciation of the threats that may threaten the company's position can also be achieved. Adopting a customer-focused view of strengths and weaknesses helps to ensure that realistic decisions are made about where to direct resources, helping the business to make the best of the available opportunities.

A3 Checklist: SWOT Analysis – Strengths, Weaknesses, Opportunities and Threats

Please read and complete the following checklist.

1. What you should have found out:

Before moving on to the next chapter you should have developed a SWOT analysis for each market. To achieve this, you must have understood the strengths and weaknesses which are generated by internal issues and have identified the opportunities and threats arising out of external environmental conditions. You must also have used ranking to show the relative importance of each strength, weakness, opportunity and threat. The implications of the SWOT analysis to the business must have been recorded. If you are operating in more than one market, you will need to fill in copies of the relevant forms for each.

If you have not yet collected the necessary information to achieve this, it is vital that you return to this chapter as soon as possible and definitely prior to determining target market priorities and positioning strategies.

2. Chart which should have been completed:

Make a record of your progress in completing the following chart:

	Status of Analysis		
	Complete	Partly filled	Not complete
A3.1: The SWOT analysis	❏	❏	❏

Be prepared to revisit this chart if/when further relevant information becomes available.

3. Information collected:

The following areas of information are relevant to this chapter. Please indicate your progress in collecting this and other relevant information:

	Information		
	Collected	Collection under way	Not collected
INTERNAL ISSUES			
Marketing	❏	❏	❏
Engineering and product development	❏	❏	❏
Operations	❏	❏	❏
People	❏	❏	❏
Management	❏	❏	❏
Company resources	❏	❏	❏
Other.	❏	❏	❏
EXTERNAL ISSUES			
Legal forces	❏	❏	❏
Regulatory forces	❏	❏	❏
Political forces	❏	❏	❏
Societal (cultural) forces	❏	❏	❏
Economic conditions	❏	❏	❏
Technological forces	❏	❏	❏
Competition	❏	❏	❏
Supplier influence/power	❏	❏	❏
Customer buying power	❏	❏	❏
Other	❏	❏	❏

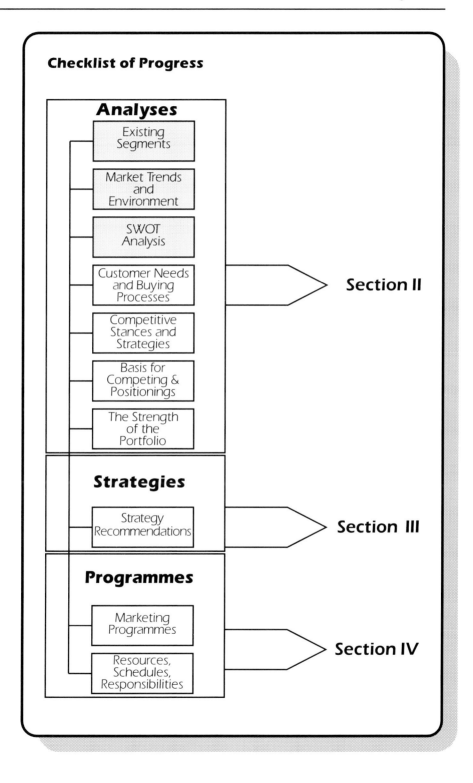

Analyses 4

Customer Needs, Expectations and Buying Processes

A4.1 Introduction

Companies often find that they must cater for the needs of a wide range of customer types. Satisfying so varied a customer base involves having a sound understanding of what product, sales and marketing attributes customers expect and need. Companies vary in their ability to track customer histories and figures; even those which regularly update such records often fail to understand fully why customers make or do not make a particular purchase.

In order to develop marketing programmes which strongly appeal to target customers, it is vital that companies fully appreciate the needs of their customer base. This means understanding the number, types and characteristics of customers in a particular market, reviewing the buying process and influences on each customer type, keeping an eye on emerging trends and identifying current perceptions of different brands and patterns of supplier loyalty. Without this understanding of buyer behaviour, it is impossible rigorously to attempt any segmentation process.

Keeping historical records of customer numbers and types has already been reviewed in chapter A1 of this workbook while sub-section A6.2 will deal with reviewing customer perceptions of competing products and brands. By the end of this chapter you will have reviewed customer characteristics, considered the buying process, buying centre and mechanics which customers go through when they buy, looked at the factors which impact upon the buying decision and re-examined the product/service requirements (Key Customer Values or KCVs) of different customer types. This chapter's analyses are the key to the segmentation process.

A4.2 Understanding Customers

A clear understanding of customer needs and requirements is central to any segmentation or marketing strategy. After all, the marketing concept is all about ensuring that the customer is the focus of decision-making. Furthermore, market segmentation itself is necessary because of the diversity of needs displayed by different customers. If companies are to capitalise on customer needs and take advantage of marketing opportunities, a detailed profile of those requirements is vital. For example, it is essential to understand the precise mix of product characteristics, service support, pricing and payment terms and delivery required by each type of customer. Any uncertainty in these areas will probably result in less effective segmentation strategies and marketing programmes being developed.

When reviewing the needs of different customer types the following questions may be helpful:

- What benefits is the customer seeking from the product or service? How tangible or intangible are these benefits?
- Does the customer have any other needs which are related to the product or service in question? How do these needs affect the purchase decision?
- Is the purchase of any other product or service linked with that being reviewed? For example, the sales of washing detergents and fabric conditioners are linked.
- What criteria does the customer consider when making the purchase decision? For example, how important are issues such as quality, delivery, service, price, product range and product innovation in the decision?
- What supplier criteria does the customer use when choosing what to buy?
- How does the customer go about searching for product or service information? For example, which media, publications, trade shows and exhibitions, word-of-mouth recommendations are used?

A4.2.1 Key Customer Values (KCVs)

Some of these questions relate specifically to customer needs or Key Customer Values (KCVs) as they are sometimes known: those factors expected and considered most important by customers. Others will prove helpful when marketing programmes are designed for different customer segments.

An understanding of KCVs is fundamental to the segmentation process and, indeed, to marketing. KCVs include anything demanded or deemed most important by target customers. For example, environmentally safe products, technical innovation, widespread distribution, warranties, low retail price, know-how support. One construction equipment manufacturer knew its customers needed a product which dug holes or transported debris. Managers did not know why customers preferred certain products in set situations, nor why various brands were considered. Some rudimentary surveying established a whole host of KCVs not previously acknowledged by the company's sales and marketing personnel: many of these attributes were already supplied but not emphasised in marketing activity, while other KCVs had to be incorporated in product and service reviews.

For existing customer groups, you have summarised these KCVs in Chart A1.1.

A4.2.2 Customer Profiles

The design of effective marketing programmes is also contingent upon having a clear profile of the characteristics of different customer types. The importance of *profiling* and using *descriptor* variables in segmentation analysis has been explained in sub-section A2.2. Many companies find that it is helpful to sketch a brief profile of key customer types formally at the same time as developing a list of key customer values. The idea that certain customer characteristics are linked with specific needs and requirements is, after all, a central concept in segmentation analysis and effective target marketing.

When this sketch analysis was carried out recently in an agro-chemicals business, a segment was identified which was typified by the 'spreadsheet farmer': under 45 years of age, profit-orientated, business-trained, technically innovative, environmentally aware, con-tinuously revising crop portfolios, and shrewd!

In a second example, two petrol retailers had apparently very similar customers, brand values and forecourt networks. There were, however, some subtle differences but over time, sales and marketing personnel had lost sight of these. In order to re-establish any differences in the minds of its executives, one company researched profiles of its customers and those of its big rival. Although both companies had a common core of customers, one company's profile included unmar-ried, younger, aggressive XR3 drivers who listened to Guns & Roses and held strong career aspirations; the second company's profile included a large number of older customers, with conservative values, 2.4 children and a Range Rover for the weekends! Although deliberately stilted, these profiles helped the company undertaking the exercise to fine-tune its promotional message and modify its merchandising in its forecourt shops. It is always important to have a clear picture of who the target customers are in each segment.

A4.2.3 Buying Process and Influences

Selling organisations must also properly understand how and why individual customers and organisations buy. This is particularly relevant given that the mechanics of buying tend to impact on the nature of the KCVs required. Understanding the buying process and the mechanics of buying steps helps companies to gear their marketing efforts to more effectively influence the buying decision. In short, this allows a more suitable marketing mix (product, price, promotion, distribution, people) to be developed for the customers targeted.

For one segment in a chemicals market, the customers (businesses) were characterised by central purchasing, expert buyers, senior level of decision-making with strong negotiating power. The mechanics of the buying process were:

a) authorisation within the customer for its purchasing personnel to negotiate with suppliers and place orders;

b) technical sampling;

c) technical approval by the customer's laboratory personnel;

d) trial production run;

e) purchasing negotiations involving senior management and purchasing officers in the customer;

f) placement of order; and

g) post-delivery on-going review of supplier.

The influences within this sequence were numerous, but *included* end-user requirements, legislation and federal laws in terms of production processes and disposal of waste products, competitive rivalry, market price, supplier innovation in product purity and methods for transporting supplies, trade bodies' gossip, and a major annual international conference. Not all factors influenced each stage in the buying process.

Buying processes have long been understood and researched (sub-section A4.3), but in segmentation it is not only important to understand the thought processes of target customers, but also the 'mechanical' steps taken in buying. Chart A4.1 (p. 69), therefore, examines thought processes and these steps. The following brief overview of the typical buying processes as presented in the literature on buyer behaviour will help provide the necessary background for filling in this chart.

A4.3 **Customer Buyer Behaviour**

When discussing the behaviour and buying mechanics of customers, it is necessary to distinguish between individual and organisational buyers. Thus consumer buyer behaviour is said to be the decision processes and acts of individuals (the end-consumers) involved in buying and using products. Organisational buyer behaviour is said to represent the purchase behaviour of other producers and re-sellers, government units and institutions. The customer portfolios of companies always vary in terms of the types of customers which are included and some businesses sell to consumers and to other organisations.

A4.3.1 Consumer Buying Decision Process

There have been many attempts to model or map out the way that individuals buy. Figure A4.1 illustrates a format which is typical of those which have been developed:

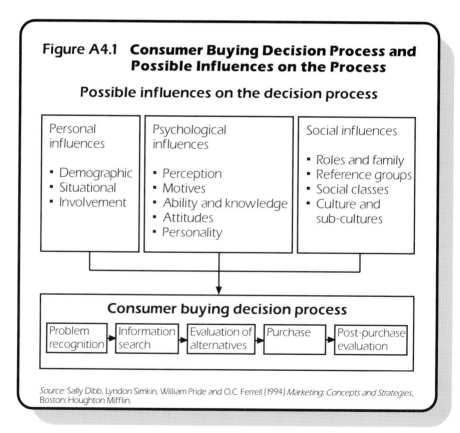

Figure A4.1   Consumer Buying Decision Process and Possible Influences on the Process

Possible influences on the decision process

Personal influences
- Demographic
- Situational
- Involvement

Psychological influences
- Perception
- Motives
- Ability and knowledge
- Attitudes
- Personality

Social influences
- Roles and family
- Reference groups
- Social classes
- Culture and sub-cultures

Consumer buying decision process

Problem recognition → Information search → Evaluation of alternatives → Purchase → Post-purchase evaluation

Source: Sally Dibb, Lyndon Simkin, William Pride and O.C. Ferrell (1994) *Marketing: Concepts and Strategies,* Boston: Houghton Mifflin.

Briefly, the consumer buying decision process suggests that consumers first recognise a problem or need for a product or service; they then search for information about relevant options (based on previous experiences, memory, KCVs, media and marketing influences); options are then evaluated against the KCVs/benchmarks set by each consumer; and the purchase is made (quickly for a routine purchase and with more care for a risky, expensive, or infrequently replaced item). The process does not end there, though, as rational consumers constantly assess the performance and suitability of their purchase: such views will influence the eventual replacement/renewal purchase.

There are a number of factors which *influence* the way in which people buy. By understanding the range of these factors, companies are in a better position to develop marketing programmes which cater for the consumers. These influencing factors can be grouped in the following way:

- *Personal influences.* Demographic issues (age/sex/occupation/income), situational factors (external conditions which exist when a purchase is made) and level of involvement.
- *Psychological influences.* Consumers' different perceptions, motives and attitudes towards what and how they purchase. Many consumers, for example, are currently motivated by 'green' environmental concerns.
- *Social influences.* Purchases made by consumers are influenced by a range of social factors. For example, individual tastes are influenced by social class and culture. Similarly, how consumers behave is affected by family roles and reference groups (friends/colleagues).

A4.3.2 The Organisational (Business-to-Business) Decision Process

Organisational markets can be classified into industrial or producer markets, re-seller markets, institutional markets and government markets. The first two types tend to deal in physical goods while the second two are more typically concerned with the provision of services.

- *Industrial or producer markets.* These companies buy products for use in the manufacture of other products or to support that manufacture. For example, Nestlé buys glucose syrup/cocoa powder/sugar, etc.

- *Re-seller markets.* Companies in this category buy goods for re-sale to customers. Generally they do not alter the physical nature of those goods. For example wholesalers or retailers, such as Marks and Spencer's or Aldi.
- *Institutional markets.* Companies in this category include charities, libraries, hospitals, colleges.
- *Government markets.* This category includes both local and national government.

This distinction into organisational type is important because it affects the characteristics of the buying process. For instance, government markets are known for their bureaucratic buying processes – often operating through a series of committees seeking tenders, taking many months.

Various attempts have been made to model the organisational buying decision process. Figure A4.2 is typical of the approaches which have been developed.

There are obvious similarities between the business-to-business and consumer buying decision processes. However, business-to-business transactions tend to be more formal. Once a need is recognised for a product or service, a specification is drawn up prior to a screening of potential suppliers. Those short-listed suppliers are ranked and assessed in terms of costs, reliability/reputation, product know-how, service levels, etc. There is also an element of post-purchase evaluation, even when regular contracts are instigated.

As with the consumer buying process there is a range of factors which impact on and *influence* the nature of buying and how that buying takes place. These include:

- *Environmental*: such as laws, regulations, economic conditions, social issues, competitive forces and technological change. For example, the impact of 1992 EC deregulation and more freedom to buy.
- *Organisational*: including company objectives (which may be short or long term), purchasing policies (such as the now outdated 'Buy British' campaign), resources, and the structure of the buying centre.
- *Interpersonal*: anyone involved in buying for an organisation will understand the power of relationships, conflict and co-operation which can impact on the decisions made.
- *Individual*: as in consumer buying, individual factors such as age, education level and job status will have an impact on the choices which are made.

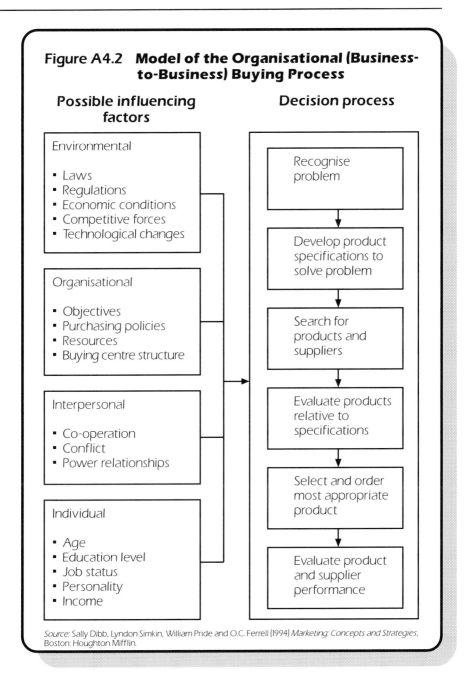

Figure A4.2 Model of the Organisational (Business-to-Business) Buying Process

Possible influencing factors

Decision process

Environmental

- Laws
- Regulations
- Economic conditions
- Competitive forces
- Technological changes

Organisational

- Objectives
- Purchasing policies
- Resources
- Buying centre structure

Interpersonal

- Co-operation
- Conflict
- Power relationships

Individual

- Age
- Education level
- Job status
- Personality
- Income

Recognise problem

↓

Develop product specifications to solve problem

↓

Search for products and suppliers

↓

Evaluate products relative to specifications

↓

Select and order most appropriate product

↓

Evaluate product and supplier performance

Source: Sally Dibb, Lyndon Simkin, William Pride and O.C. Ferrell (1994) *Marketing: Concepts and Strategies,* Boston: Houghton Mifflin.

A4.3.3 Comparing Organisational and Consumer Buyer Behaviour

There are, however, a number of obvious contrasts between consumer buying behaviour and the behaviour exhibited by businesses. These can be shown by highlighting the particular characteristics of organisational buyer behaviour.

Group Activity

Generally more people are involved in organisational buying behaviour than in consumer buying behaviour. Those involved in buying in an organisational situation are collectively referred to as the *Buying Centre* and each individual will be responsible for particular buying roles. The number of people involved in buying will be organisation-specific, but usually relates to the type of purchase being made, the risk associated with it and time pressure.

High Risk

Buying for organisations is usually more high risk than a consumer purchase. Risk in organisational purchases can come from high product value, the possible consequences of purchase, lack of knowledge about the product or service being bought, and uncertainty about the buying process or how to deal with suppliers.

Fewer and Larger Buyers

Fast Moving Consumer Goods (FMCG) companies tend to aim their products at mass markets but many companies in organisational markets are reliant on relatively few customers. This means there is a tendency for long-term relationships to be developed, with companies seeking the benefits of reduced risk, trust, mutual adaptation, time saving, etc., and there is more use of personal selling (face-to-face contact).

Formal Buying Process

Organisational buyers are often restricted by certain company rules/procedures and have a fairly limited say in the purchase which is made. Some organisations are particularly bureaucratic. Generally, there is extensive use of formal quotes and tendering.

Nature of Demand

Demand in organisational markets is derived from demand for products or services in consumer markets. This means it tends to fluctuate according to the level of demand for consumer goods (e.g. the demand for glucose syrup is affected by the demand for confectionery).

Geographic Concentration of Buyers

There is a tendency for concentration of certain industries to occur in different areas. For example, in the UK IT suppliers are now centred on the M4 motorway corridor.

A4.4 Recording Key Customer Values (KCVs), Buying Processes and Influences

At this stage in the analysis it is necessary to add to the historical and quantitative picture of customers developed in chapter A1. For each type or group of customers a more qualitative profile is needed. Using a copy of Chart A4.1 for *each customer group or segment*, make a record of:

(i) *The Buying Process Mechanics.* List the steps involved in the buying process (from the customer's viewpoint). What steps does the customer go through in order to make the purchase?

(ii) *The Buying Centre.* List the members of the buying centre. This list should include all individuals who have a role in any stage of buying and should indicate the nature of that role.

(iii) *The Core Influences.* Record any factors which have an influence on the buying decision being made. Which factors/issues influence *each* step in the process described (see (i))?

(iv) *Customer Profile.* Build up a picture of the typical characteristics of the customer type under review. Include any relevant personality, demographic, location, situational details.

(v) *Key Customer Values.* Make a list of the KCVs (needs) required by each customer group.

The details which you have recorded in Chart A4.1 will have important implications for your business. Record your impressions of these implications by answering the question in Chart A4.2. For example, it is often helpful to identify at which stages in the buying process competitors are active with their marketing and which influencing factors they seek to address. Can any lessons be learned from competitors' activity in the buying processes of customers?

Chart A4.1 is perhaps the most important in this workbook. Commence by filling in one chart per existing customer group (as defined previously in Chart A1.1). It is likely that you and your colleagues feel it is not possible to generalise the customer profile for a particular pre-determined customer group. In this case, split this group until sub-groups can be profiled. Similarly, if KCVs and buying processes cannot readily be summarised for a particular customer group, it is likely that dissimilar customers have been 'shoe-horned' in together for convenience purposes. If this approach is allowed to continue, these analyses will not determine market segments. If at each stage in completing Chart A4.1 generalisations are not easy for a pre-defined customer group, be prepared to look for sub-groups: sets of customers who do share similar profiles, who have shared KCVs and who buy in a similar manner. Although at this stage, this may result in a proliferation of customer groups, as described later in the Strategy Section of this workbook, subsequently 'similar' sub-groups can be regrouped if they share common KCVs and buying profiles.

One company had historically broken its customers into groups dependent on type of product purchased from it, irrespective of what KCVs its customers had, who they were, where they were located, who the end-users were, market trends, competitive activity, etc. There were eight customer groups based on the company's own product groups. In completing this Chart A4.1, one of the eight was felt to be in reality five separate customer groups, a second was broken down into four groups, a third into six groups, and so on: based on customer profiles, KCVs and buying processes. Eventually, this led to thirty-five customer groups. When the overall picture was re-evaluated, regrouping *across* the company's product groups and across customer industries, resulted in fourteen market segments. In each of these fourteen segments, customers had similar needs and buying processes. Even prior to this stage, the breakdown into sub-groups had revealed sets of customers whose needs had been ignored and where there was significant sales potential – the company's original aggregating of customers had wrongly played down their importance.

Chart A4.1 Customers, KCVs, Buying Process Steps and Core Influences

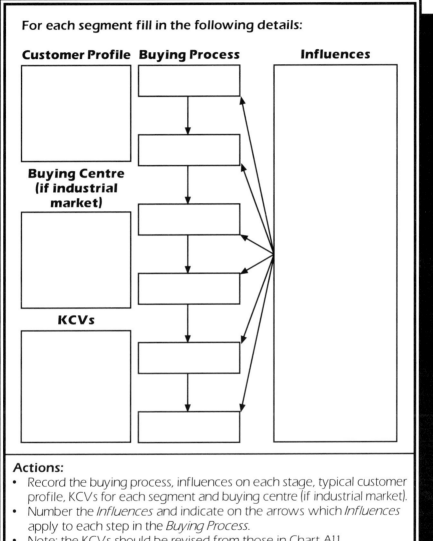

For each segment fill in the following details:

Customer Profile **Buying Process** **Influences**

Buying Centre (if industrial market)

KCVs

Actions:
- Record the buying process, influences on each stage, typical customer profile, KCVs for each segment and buying centre (if industrial market).
- Number the *Influences* and indicate on the arrows which *Influences* apply to each step in the *Buying Process*.
- Note: the KCVs should be revised from those in Chart A1.1.

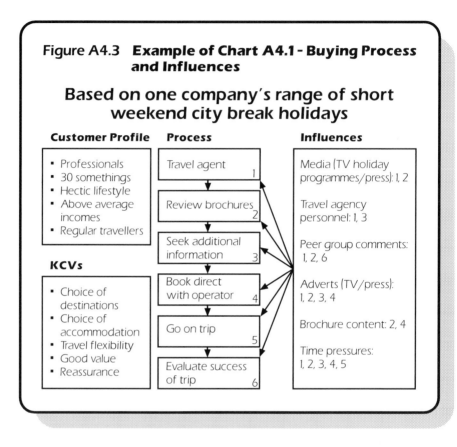

Figure A4.3 **Example of Chart A4.1 - Buying Process and Influences**

Based on one company's range of short weekend city break holidays

Customer Profile

- Professionals
- 30 somethings
- Hectic lifestyle
- Above average incomes
- Regular travellers

KCVs

- Choice of destinations
- Choice of accommodation
- Travel flexibility
- Good value
- Reassurance

Process

Travel agent   1

Review brochures   2

Seek additional information   3

Book direct with operator   4

Go on trip   5

Evaluate success of trip   6

Influences

Media (TV holiday programmes/press): 1, 2

Travel agency personnel: 1, 3

Peer group comments: 1, 2, 6

Adverts (TV/press): 1, 2, 3, 4

Brochure content: 2, 4

Time pressures: 1, 2, 3, 4, 5

Chart A4.2 Implications from Examining the Buying Process and KCVs

At which stages in the buying process are competitors active?
Are competitors maximising opportunities currently missed by the business? If so, which ones?
Implications? Are there any additional stages in the buying process the business should try to affect?
Which influencing factors can the business in turn influence?
Are there any edges over competitors in the stages already tackled by the business or influences addressed?

Actions:
- The principal benefit of the analysis in Chart A4.1 is to provoke the information used later on in the Strategy Section of this workbook to redefine segments, so the ramifications of the analysis in Chart A4.1 must be considered.
- There are, though, additional benefits in terms of learning from competitors' activities within the buying process and in addressing the influencing factors; there are edges the business will have over these rivals, plus there will be stages and people currently not targeted by the business who must be.

A4.5 Summary

This chapter helps to develop an understanding of customers' buying behaviour. This important area of marketing analysis, which companies frequently overlook, provides valuable insight into customer needs which goes further than simply considering product requirements. By examining the mechanisms of buying it is possible to develop an entire marketing offering which is geared to satisfying customer requirements from the point at which an unfulfilled need is recognised right up to the point of consumption. An appreciation of the core influences on buying should assist the business in determining which of these influences it is important to control. This additional understanding can be particularly important in markets where there is little variety in product needs or where competition is especially intense. In these circumstances using buying behaviour characteristics to distinguish between different customer groups may offer an opportunity for developing a differential advantage.

A4 Checklist: Customer Needs, Expectations and Buying Processes

Please read and complete the following checklist.

1. What you should have found out:

Before moving on to the next chapter you should have a clear understanding of the buying behaviour of each of your groups of customers. This means understanding the mechanics/steps which customers go through when purchasing your product. You should also have described the influencing factors which impact upon buying, have listed the members of the buying centre (if in an industrial market) and described typical profiles of each customer type. Key Customer Values (KCVs) should also have been listed. Finally, the implications of what you have discovered and recorded should have been explored.

If you have not yet collected the necessary information to achieve this, it is unlikely you will be able to progress. Without this information, you cannot redefine segments or fully understand the customer needs and purchasing behaviour fundamental to segmentation.

2. Charts which should have been completed:

Make a record of your progress completing the following charts:

	Status of Analysis		
	Complete	Partly filled	Not complete
A4.1: Customers, KCVs, buying process steps & core influences	❏	❏	❏
A4.2: Implications of the buying process	❏	❏	❏

Be prepared to revisit these charts if/when further relevant information becomes available. Progress can only be superficial until these charts have been comprehensively completed.

3. Information collected:

The following areas of information are relevant to this chapter. Please indicate your progress in collecting this and other relevant information:

	Information		
	Collected	Collection under way	Not collected
Segment by segment buying process steps	❏	❏	❏
Segment by segment core influencing factors	❏	❏	❏
Segment by segment profiles	❏	❏	❏
Segment by segment KCV summary	❏	❏	❏
Other.	❏	❏	❏

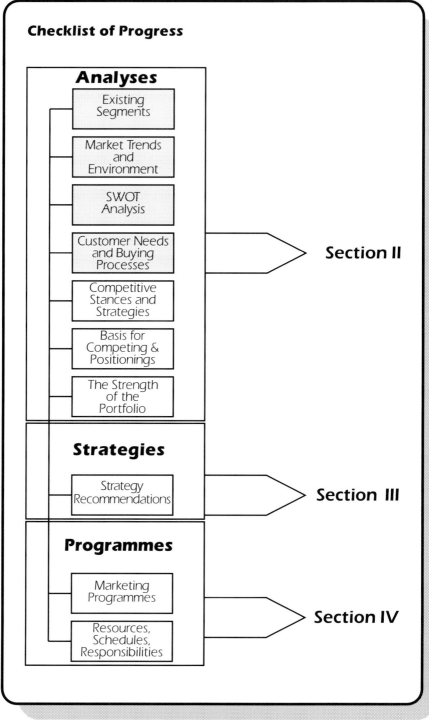

Analyses 5

Competition I – Competitive Stances and Strategies

A5.1 Introduction

Decisions about marketing strategy must fully consider the prevailing competitive situation in which a company operates. There seems little doubt that marketing success is closely linked with becoming 'competitor-orientated'. Not surprisingly, successful market segmentation also relies on having a sound understanding of competitors' relative strengths and weaknesses, market shares and positionings. By combining an appreciation of the competitive situation with key customer needs, companies are better able to pinpoint attractive segments and position their product offerings. Closely monitoring change in the competitive arena helps companies maintain control over their segmentation strategy.

This chapter reviews the characteristics of the competitive arena in which companies operate, examines the industry forces which are present and considers the competitive positions which different players can adopt. By the end of this chapter you will have developed an overview of the competitive arena in which your business operates. This will involve identifying the stances occupied by key competitors in each segment, recording market share and the key customer values which each player aims to satisfy and identifying where competitors have a unique advantage.

A5.2 Understanding the Competitive Arena

American management guru Michael Porter considers the competitive arena to consist of competing organisations jockeying for position in an environment determined by a number of outside forces (see Figure A5.1). Within this arena the jockeying for position among competing organisations is influenced by the threat of new market entrants, the bargaining power of customers, the threat of substitute products or services and the bargaining power of suppliers.

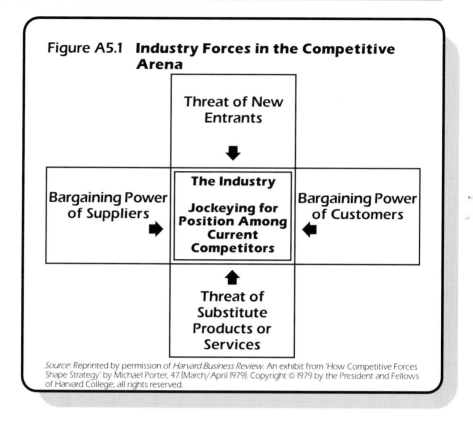

Figure A5.1 **Industry Forces in the Competitive Arena**

Bargaining Power of Suppliers

The degree to which a particular supplier impacts on the situation depends on the availability of alternative suppliers and product substitutes. In monopoly situations the bargaining power of the supplier is particularly high and may be associated with high prices and inflexible, poor quality, product offerings. At the other extreme, supplying companies in industries with many suppliers and much substitution frequently have quite low bargaining power.

Bargaining Power of Buyers

High buyer bargaining power usually occurs in industries where suppliers' power is low and where large volumes of standardised items can readily be sourced elsewhere. In many cases these items form only a part of the final product.

Threat of Substitute Products or Services

A proliferation of substitute products within an industry can significantly limit the growth potential and long-term profits. This results in competing companies having less control over price and possibly facing over-capacity problems.

Threat of New Entrants

New entrants in a market give increased capacity which can limit the market share or profits of existing competitors. The likely impact of new entrants is determined in part by any barriers to entry. Typical barriers to entry include the presence of strongly branded competitors, economies of scale, control of distribution and high capital requirements. In markets where barriers are high, the number of new entrants will be limited.

Porter believes there are three bases on which a business can compete. An organisation which *fails* to master any one of these is *un*likely to have the strengths with which to fend off competitors:

- *Cost leadership*: Low cost base through scale economies.
- *Differentiation*: Unique product or marketing offer: innovative product, service, branding, distribution or pricing.
- *Focus*: Often smaller companies unable to opt for *cost* or *differentiation* – specialisation in tightly defined markets.

No matter how it is analysed or described, the nature of competition must be understood for effective marketing management. In terms of segmentation, without a grasp of the competitive arena, the threats, the opportunities and relative strengths of key players, it is not possible to identify the segments most likely to be the essential priorities for the business.

One organisation, operating in the pharmaceuticals sector, naively believed it knew all about its rivals. In terms of products, sales volumes and geographic coverage, it did. However, new sales initiatives and promotional activity often caught management unawares. Even after lengthy trials, new product launches were frequently a surprise. Competitive reaction was never considered when sales and marketing drives were developed. The competition, though, was surprisingly predictable in its reaction and rivals' activity should have been considered and pre-empted during the formulation of the business's own plans.

A UK supermarket chain analysed its UK rivals comprehensively, but not companies in Europe. Today, its leading threats come from

German and Scandinavian retail chains which are strongly challenging its market leadership. Lack of competitive knowledge delayed the UK company's response. One southern European construction equipment manufacturer has found that today's threat is posed by Japanese micro-bore tunnelling robots and not from European, Japanese and American manufacturers of earth digging equipment.

A knowledge of competition is essential: who the key players are, their respective market positions and intentions, the customer needs they service, and any unique advantages they possess. The use of warfare analogies is a useful means of addressing these issues. This approach is discussed in sub-section A5.3; Chart A5.1 provides a suitable intelligence gathering format. The understanding of customers' perceptions of competing brands is featured in sub-section A6.3.

A5.3 Warfare Strategies

The analysis of competition and the development of competitive strategies have also been linked to military principles. Under this scenario, competing companies represent the *enemy* which must be defeated. In any market there are said to be five different types of competitive position which companies can occupy. Which position a company occupies, and how this fits in with what the competition is doing, will impact on the strategy which that company should follow.

A5.3.1 Competitive Positions

There are five possible positions for an organisation to adopt.

- *Market Leader.* This is the highest market share company which retains its position by trying to expand the total market, perhaps by finding new uses for a product, or increasing market share (market penetration), for example through an aggressive advertising campaign. It is necessary for these companies to achieve a balance between aggressively seeking new market share while protecting their existing position.
- *Market Challenger.* This position is occupied by one or more non-market leaders which *aggressively* attack for additional market share.
- *Fast Movers.* These are not the major players in a market, but they are growing and attempting to win share. They will not in the short-

term challenge for leadership, but they are gaining at the expense of rivals.

- *Market Follower.* These are low share competitors without the resources/market position/R&D/commitment to challenge or seriously contend for market leadership. Instead they are happy to settle for a smaller share of the market: the 'me-toos'.
- *Market Nicher.* Companies which specialise in terms of market/ product/customers by finding a safe, profitable market segment. As markets mature, increasing competitiveness forces larger rivals to target such segments, making life difficult for the nicher. Companies which commit all their resources to one niche market can find themselves particularly susceptible in such circumstances.

Why are competitive positions important? Quite simply, different marketing strategies are appropriate depending upon the competitive position. Nichers specialise and are narrowly focused. Market leaders have to fend off competitors' attacks while continuing plans to develop and grow their markets. Challengers are aggressive but must only attack the leader's and other challengers' weak points: head-on moves will most likely be costly. Followers are the 'me-toos' in the marketplace: they copy other players' successes and may lack the strength to compete aggressively. Fast movers need to be countered, and will seriously harm the smaller players in a market. The various marketing strategies may be based either on attacking or defensive moves.

A5.3.2 Principles of Defensive Warfare Strategies

The skill to adopt a defensive position is important if companies are to protect their existing market share. However, defence should not be regarded solely as a negative activity. Strong defence involves striking a balance between waiting to be attacked and responding to aggressive competitive moves. In general, only the market leader should consider adopting a defensive role, but even for this player, it is essential to combine defensive and offensive strategies. Some companies fall into a false sense of security about their market position and leave themselves open to attack from aggressive market challengers. Such companies should remember that adopting a defensive position does not necessarily mean remaining static; they should be ready to move and respond to aggressive marketing effort from competitors. Defence still presents several options:

- Build walls around strong positions. This requires companies to fully understand their true strengths (for example brand name), and to be proactive in their attempts to retain those strengths.
- Protect weak areas. Attention on weak areas can sometimes be diverted by marketing tactics which focus on other aspects of the product/marketing offering.
- Be mobile and ready to move. Companies should be quick to exploit new markets, products and opportunities.
- Withdrawal from market/product if absolutely necessary. It can be sensible to consolidate in areas which are strong, thus focusing resources. Such action should not leave weak areas which might allow competitors access to key markets.

A5.3.3 Principles of Offensive Warfare Strategies

The principles of offensive warfare are particularly relevant to companies in a non-market leading position, which are challenging aggressively for additional market share. It is often regarded as lower risk to attack market followers and market nichers rather than the market leading organisation, but this depends on the strength of the leader's position. Attacking companies must beware the dangers of antagonising powerful, resource-rich market leaders. If the leader is to be attacked, the challenging organisation must find a weakness in the leader's strength and attack at that point. Launching the attack on a narrow front tends to increase the chances of success. The challenger should be sure that it has the resources to sustain the attack for as long as necessary.

- *Head to head.* This full-frontal method of attack is in many ways the most difficult to sustain and only the most powerful challengers should attempt it. The attack involves attempting to match the market leader blow by blow on some aspect of the marketing programme (for example, price). Challengers who attempt this approach often fail!
- *Attack weak points.* This approach to attack requires the challenger to identify and match its key areas of strength and weakness against the market leader. Efforts can then be pitched against points of particular weakness.
- *Adopt a multi-pronged strategy.* It can be appropriate to overwhelm competitors, with several points of attack (for example combining a promotional programme with product innovation) and thus

diluting competitors' ability to respond.

- *Guerrilla attack*. This type of challenge is not large-scale or prolonged. The intention is to annoy competitors with unpredictable and periodic attacks.

A5.3.4 Strategies for Market Followers and Nichers

Although there are opportunities for *followers* in markets, as Amstrad showed in the personal computer market, companies occupying these positions are often vulnerable to attack from their larger competitors. In order to minimise the risks of such attack, market followers (and businesses with low shares as *fast movers*) should use market segmentation carefully, concentrating only on areas where the company can cope. It is also helpful to specialise rather than diversify so that resources are not spread too thinly. This means the emphasis is on profitability rather than sales growth. Using R&D as efficiently as possible can also help ensure that resources are used in the most appropriate manner.

In many markets, *nichers* are the most vulnerable competitors. They must avoid competition with other organisations in order to ensure their success, particularly as markets become more mature. This can be achieved by seeking safe market segments, typically in areas where big companies do not believe it is worth competing. Such niches may be secured by specialising on a particular market, customer or marketing mix. However, nichers must avoid becoming over committed to one small area of the market. This can be achieved by being strong in more than one niche. If there is an aggressive attack on one niche segment, this means that there may be opportunities to switch resources to another.

A5.4 Monitoring Competitors' Strategies

No matter what the market is, it clearly is of fundamental importance to gain an idea of competitors' strategies. It is not too difficult to review past actions, competitors' product launches, price campaigns, distribution policies, promotional campaigns, press releases; their reaction to the business's product launches or modifications to sales and marketing programmes. Many companies are surprisingly predictable. As with the marketing environment, however, many managers know a lot about their competitors – from chance discussions, press comment, industry gossip, dealer feedback, the sales force – but often such insights simply are not shared with colleagues until it is too late. With an ear to the ground, much competitive marketing intelligence can be gathered at low cost:

- product and pricing activities;
- dealer and customer service moves;
- key account moves;
- likely reaction to the business's moves; and
- reactions to changes in the trading environment.

A5.5 Recording Competitors

It is important to recognise the market leader and strongest challengers, plus those companies occupying the other competitive positions. As detailed in sub-section A4.2, it is important to know what product, sales and marketing attributes customers expect and need. In terms of a competitor analysis, it is also important to know which Key Customer Values (KCVs) each competitor is believed to be able to match/service, and whether in so doing any competitor gains a differential or competitive advantage in the marketplace over its rivals. A differential advantage (DA) – or competitive edge – is something desired by the target market which only the company or its product has; it is not currently readily matched by rival companies or products (sub-section A6.2 discusses DAs further).

Chart A5.1 provides a suitable summary grid per segment which:

1. aggregates information regarding the competitors and positions occupied within each segment;

2. considers the KCVs met or offered by *competitors*; and

3. examines whether the KCVs delivered in each segment constitute a differential/competitive advantage.

Chart A5.1 **Competitive Positions and Differential Advantage Overview**

Competitive Position	Segment:	Segment:	Segment:
Market Leader: • Market Share Change • KCVs Offered • DA (if any)	- - - - -	- - - - -	- - - - -
Challenger 1: • Market Share Change • KCVs Offered • DA (if any)	- - - - -	- - - - -	- - - - -
Challenger 2: • Market Share Change • KCVs Offered • DA (if any)	- - - - -	- - - - -	- - - - -
Challenger 3: • Market Share Change • KCVs Offered • DA (if any)	- - - - -	- - - - -	- - - - -
Fast Mover: • Market Share Change • KCVs Offered • DA (if any)	- - - - -	- - - - -	- - - - -
Follower: • Market Share Change • KCVs Offered • DA (if any)	- - - - -	- - - - -	- - - - -
Nicher: • Market Share change • KCVs Offered • DA (if any)	- - - - -	- - - - -	- - - - -

Actions:
- Record the competitive positions for each segment.
- The KCVs on this chart are those KCVs that each competitor is able to match.
- Most companies do not have a DA (differential advantage), so this slot may be left blank for many companies.
- There is *no* need to list actual %s for market share changes, current year versus last year. Key to market share entries: ++ large market share increase; + small market share increase; − small market share decline; −− large market share decline.

Figure A5.2 Example of Chart A5.1 - Competitive Positions and Differential Advantage

Competitive Position	Segment: Custom Compounders
Market Leader: ▪ **Market Share Change** ▪ **KCVs Offered** ▪ **DA (if any)**	- King Co Ltd - 36% + - Tech Approach - Supply Security - Brand/Co Size
Challenger 1: ▪ **Market Share Change** ▪ **KCVs Offered** ▪ **DA (if any)**	- Trying Hard Inc - 23% ++ - Special Grades - Tech Approach - Own Sales Force
Challenger 2: ▪ **Market Share Change** ▪ **KCVs Offered** ▪ **DA (if any)**	- Having a Go PLC - 17% + - Tech Approach - Supply Security - Plant Coverage
Challenger 3: ▪ **Market Share Change** ▪ **KCVs Offered** ▪ **DA (if any)**	- - - - -
Fast Mover: ▪ **Market Share Change** ▪ **KCVs Offered** ▪ **DA (if any)**	- Small & Trying Co - 8% ++ - Tech Approach -
Follower: ▪ **Market Share Change** ▪ **KCVs Offered** ▪ **DA (if any)**	- Mr Small Fry Inc - 4% +/− - -
Nicher: ▪ **Market Share Change** ▪ **KCVs Offered** ▪ **DA (if any)**	- Specio-Chems PLC - 3% + - Tech Approach - - Relationships
▪ **Material has been adapted from the chemicals industry.**	

A5.6 Summary

This chapter aims to build an overview of the competitive arena in which organisations operate. The impact of a business's marketing strategy is shaped by the actions of various competitive players and the way in which each strives to match key customer values. It is important to understand how competitors will react to the business's target market strategy and associated marketing programmes. No business can operate in isolation of its competitors' moves and it is vital to anticipate their reactions. Many companies behave in a surprisingly 'predictable' manner: once their activities over time have been monitored certain patterns in product launches, promotional activity, pricing policies and reactions become apparent. In assessing how competitors have behaved in recent years and in understanding how they have reacted to the business's moves in the past, it should be possible to 'second-guess' how these rivals will behave. It is also crucial to establish which KCVs each competitor is capable of servicing as this will reveal weaknesses for the business to exploit and possibly weaknesses in the business's own position to address.

A5 Checklist: Competitive Stances and Strategies

Please read and complete the following checklist.

1. What you should have found out:

Before moving on to the next chapter you should have developed an overview of the competitive arena in which your business operates. This means understanding, for each segment, which competitors may occupy the competitive positions – market leader, challenger, fast mover, follower and nicher. In addition, the market share, KCVs serviced and any differential advantage offered by each competitor should have been recorded.

If you have not yet collected the necessary information to achieve this, it is vital that you return to this chapter as soon as possible, and before determining target market priorities, positioning strategies in each segment targeted, and marketing mix recommendations.

2. Chart which should have been completed:

Make a record of your progress in completing the following chart:

	Status of Analysis		
	Complete	Partly filled	Not complete
A5.1: Competitive positions and differential advantage	❏	❏	❏

Be prepared to revisit this chart if/when further relevant information becomes available.

3. Information collected:

The following areas of information are relevant to this chapter. Please indicate your progress in collecting this and other relevant information:

	Information		
	Collected	Collection under way	Not collected
Segment by segment competitive positions	❏	❏	❏
Segment by segment market share changes for each competitor	❏	❏	❏
Competitor by competitor KCVs serviced	❏	❏	❏
Competitor by competitor DA (if any)	❏	❏	❏
Other.	❏	❏	❏

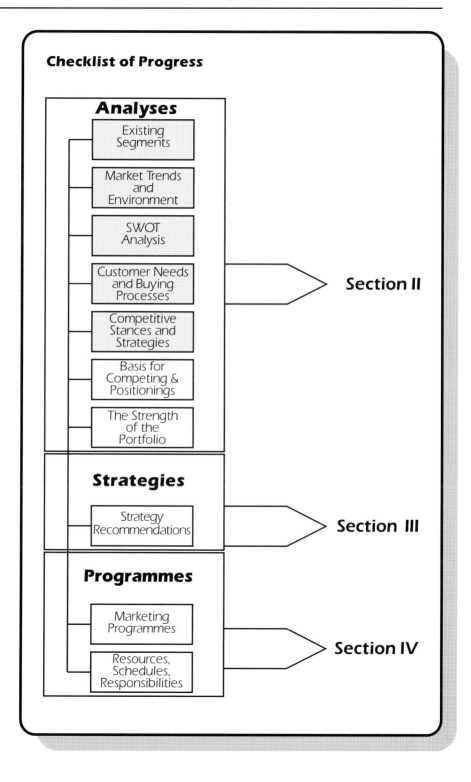

Checklist of Progress

Analyses

- Existing Segments
- Market Trends and Environment
- SWOT Analysis
- Customer Needs and Buying Processes
- Competitive Stances and Strategies
- Basis for Competing & Positionings
- The Strength of the Portfolio

> **Section II**

Strategies

- Strategy Recommendations

> **Section III**

Programmes

- Marketing Programmes
- Resources, Schedules, Responsibilities

> **Section IV**

Analyses 6

Competition II – Basis for Competing and Brand Positionings

A6.1 Introduction

Once the characteristics of the competitive arena in which a business operates have been established, the business must identify a basis for competing. A basis for competing hinges on successfully identifying a differential advantage (DA) or competitive edge. A differential advantage – or competitive edge – is something *which is highly desired by the target market customers*, which the business or its product has, which is not currently matched by rival companies or products.

This chapter reviews the steps for determining a differential advantage and discusses the differences between genuine advantages and characteristics which target customers regard as a basic entry requirement (often called 'givens'). Finally, brand positioning strategy is discussed and the concept of the perceptual/positioning map explained.

By the end of this chapter you will have identified potential advantages (strengths) for the business over rivals. In each segment you will have considered whether these advantages provide a sufficient basis for a differential advantage. You will also have developed one or more positioning maps, using some of the Key Customer Values identified earlier as axes. The business's position and the positions of all leading competitors' products/brands will have been plotted on the map(s). Finally, given the existing positions of the business and its rivals, the implications in terms of positioning strategy and required marketing programme actions will have been established.

A6.2 Basis for Competing

A6.2.1 The Importance of Developing a Differential Advantage

Without a differential advantage, success in the marketplace in the longer term is unlikely and the company will be highly vulnerable to competitors' moves. Trading may be purely on the basis of price, and in such circumstances failure in the marketplace is almost inevitable.

Companies with a genuine and sustainable differential advantage can gear their marketing programmes to emphasise the businesses' real strengths or advantages. This exerts pressure on competitors to exceed the offerings being made.

For example, Toyota stresses in its press advertising the capabilities and friendliness of its dealers; Chanel the eminence of its brands and fragrances; the AA its coverage and ability to help; 3M its innovative creativity; DHL its speed and reliability; Duracell the longevity of its cells; BA Club Europe the added service, comfort and convenience; JCB the value and reliability inherent in its brand name.

A6.2.2 *Steps in Determining a Differential Advantage*

Businesses sometimes mistakenly believe that any strength is a potential differential advantage. However, this is not always the case. Following the steps below helps establish whether or not a differential advantage really exists.

1. Identify the market's segments.

2. Establish what product and service attributes are desired and demanded by each segment or customer group.

3. Decide which of these attributes the business offers.

4. Determine which attributes the business's competitors offer.

5. Consider what the marketplace perceives the competitors' genuine strengths to be.

6. Identify whether any gaps exist between customer expectations of the product/service on offer and perceptions of the competitors' offers.

7. Consider whether any gaps identified under (6) above are matched by the business and its offerings. If the business is able to match one or more of these gaps, the potential exists for a differential advantage to be developed.

8. Question whether any of these potential advantages for the business can be emphasised through sales and marketing programmes.

9. Consider the sustainability of these advantages for the business. How easily and quickly can competitors catch up? Is it possible for

the business to defend these advantages?

10. If there are no current advantages for the business, given the gaps identified between competitors' offerings and customer expectations, consider which areas offer potential for developing a future differential advantage.

11. In order to maximise any existing or potential advantages, detail the changes which the business must make to its R&D, engineering, sales and marketing.

A6.2.3 Givens Versus Differential Advantages

Managers often identify apparent advantages which may be no more than strengths. Competitive prices, consistent quality, technical performance, delivery, brand credibility, technical support may be keen, but in reality are often matched – if not bettered – by at least some of the strongest competitors. The way to distinguish between the two is to remember that a strength is not a differential advantage or competitive edge if matched by rivals.

Similarly, an advantage or strength is not really the basis for competing in a market if in reality it is a 'given' – something expected and taken for granted by customers and dealers. Keen price, delivery on time, product quality are just some examples of attributes customers assume to be there and which are taken for granted. For example, in the market for car parts, efficient and fast delivery is a given – an expected requirement which companies must be able to provide if they are to operate in the market. A differential advantage has to go further; it must genuinely appeal to customers and be ahead of the competition's offer.

For example, a workshop for an international paints manufacturer identified these bases for competing as 'givens' – aspects either taken for granted by customers or matched by rivals:

- competitive price;
- consistent quality;
- technical performance;
- delivery;
- credibility; and
- technical support.

The determination of a real differential advantage proved harder to describe, but was eventually summed up by various points which together gave this statement of differential or competitive advantage:

> We start with *technical innovation* which we can *manufacture* and *supply globally*, backed up by *local* teams with a high level of *expertise* in *technical service*, supported by a *wide product range*. Finally, being part of a large corporation gives added credibility.

> Strong global presence – being able to talk to customers world-wide at all levels.

A differential advantage is not normally so convoluted when defined. Many companies have an edge over rivals in terms of a product's features, brand identity, channel of distribution, sales force, after-sales support or warranty, for example. Remember, unless the target customers perceive there to be an advantage over the competition, there is no differential advantage. A strength from the SWOT analysis may be part of a DA, but in itself is not the same as a DA. Internal views are an inadequate basis for determining if there is a DA: customers' impressions are the deciding factor.

Most businesses do not have a differential advantage. Even some market leaders no longer have one – their market share may be due to historical advantages. Even when a company's product and marketing do have an advantage in a segment, it is likely to be short-lived. Nevertheless, having an advantage gives a genuine edge over competitors and forces them to retaliate by going one better. Knowing where there is an advantage – and where competitors have advantages (see Chart A5.1) – helps when prioritising which segments to target. It is essential that the marketing programmes produced to implement the target market strategy emphasise any differential advantage. This is also true for the desired brand positioning (Chart A6.2): everyone must be aware of the messages to stress to customers through sales and marketing programmes.

A6.2.4 Recording Differential Advantages

For each segment determine what product/service/marketing/brand attributes are required or expected by customers and dealers. Decide which of these attributes is (or could be) offered by the business. Determine whether any of these attributes are offered by any leading competitors. If they are not, they may form the basis for a differential advantage or competitive edge for the business. These attributes wanted by target customers, provided by the business and not matched by leading rivals, must seem attractive to distributors and to customers and they must be suitable to form the core of sales and marketing programmes. Chart A6.1 provides a suitable summary for this analysis.

Chart A6.1 **Identification of DAs**

Segment Name	Identified Advantages (Strengths) for the Business Over Rivals	Are Advantages Sufficient Basis for a DA (Differential Advantage)?
1		
2		
3		
4		
5		
6		
7		
8		

Actions:
- Record any DAs held by the business.
- Remember a strength is only a possible DA if target customers desire it and rivals do not offer it.
- *Remember* that to be sufficient for a DA, the strength must be cost effective and in the short term, defensible.

A6.3 Brand and Product Positioning

A6.3.1 The Role of Brand Positionings

The positioning of a brand or product is reflected in the marketplace's perceptions of an offering's performance according to criteria which customers regard as important. These criteria may have been identified in a number of ways, including feedback from the sales force or independent marketing research. Although managers' views of how particular offerings are perceived are important, there is no substitute for identifying how *customers* and *distributors* see the brands and products compared with the strengths of competitors' offers. Before any marketing strategy can be determined or brand positioning strategy implemented it is essential that the market's perceptions are properly understood (see sub-section 2.4). It may be necessary to instigate a data collection exercise to help with this part of the process.

A6.3.2 The Positioning/Perceptual Map

There are various techniques for understanding and depicting respective brand and product positionings. The most common and one of the most user-friendly is the perceptual map, often termed the positioning map.

Perceptual mapping is based on a variety of mathematical or qualitative approaches designed to place or describe consumers' perceptions of brands or products on one or a series of 'spatial maps'. It is a means of visually depicting consumers' perceptions, showing the relative positionings of different brands or products (and thereby companies).

The core attributes must be identified through consumer research, with follow-up confirmatory research identifying the relative positionings of the brands or companies to be plotted.

For example, a perceptual map of the UK furniture market, as produced in the late 1980s by a management team, identified 'value for money' as the key attribute. Research showed that consumers were in reality more concerned with price and product quality, two different marketing mix components which, while related to value for money, needed tackling separately. A starting point may be management's views, but ultimately, the perceptual map must be based on axes and values determined by customers.

It is important for all marketers to understand the positioning of their products on such a spatial map, vis-à-vis competitors,

Figure A6.1 **A Perceptual Map for the Hotel Industry**

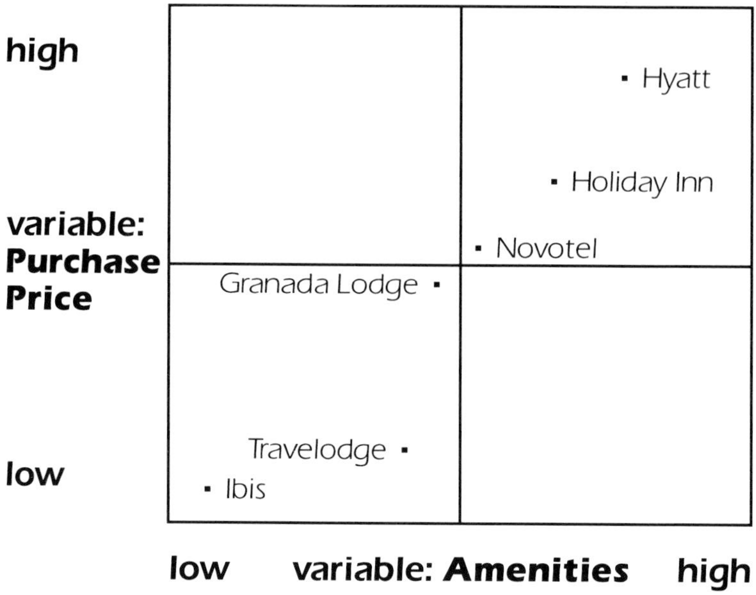

particularly in order to develop realistic and effective marketing programmes.

A6.3.3 Recording the Positioning Map

The analyses so far undertaken (see Charts A1.1, A4.1 and A5.1) have ascertained the core Key Customer Values desired or demanded by customers. This work has also presented a full list or league table of these KCVs. These variables provide a useful starting point for the positioning maps you will be developing. You should construct your first positioning map(s), per segment, using these leading KCVs as the variables for the X- and Y-axes.

The business's position should be marked on the map – or graph – along with the positions for all leading competitors' products/ brands. Remember to use data from customers and distributors to ensure that the results are as objective as possible. The relative distances between the companies indicate their ability or inability to

Chart A6.2 **The Positioning Map**

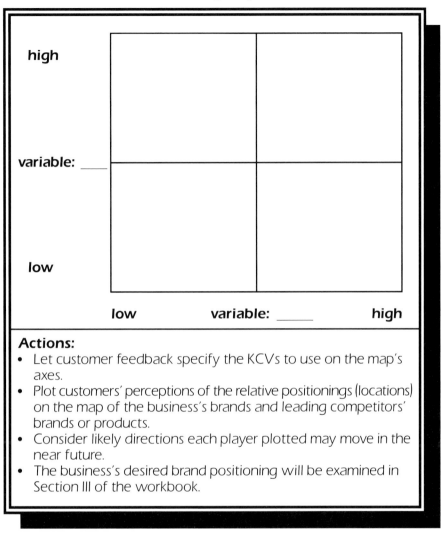

Actions:
- Let customer feedback specify the KCVs to use on the map's axes.
- Plot customers' perceptions of the relative positionings (locations) on the map of the business's brands and leading competitors' brands or products.
- Consider likely directions each player plotted may move in the near future.
- The business's desired brand positioning will be examined in Section III of the workbook.

satisfactorily match customers' needs for the main KCVs. Chart A6.2 presents a blueprint for the perceptual maps.

A6.4 Summary

This chapter has covered two areas. The first part examined the business's basis for competing, in each segment. This is considered to be the firm's differential advantage. Having a sound and sustainable differential advantage makes it easier for the business to develop effective marketing programmes. The second part of the chapter looked at the positioning of the business's products/brands within the marketplace. Positioning/perceptual maps provide a usual way of summarising the perceptions which customers have of the different product/brand offerings. Understanding the positionings of the business's and competitors' products is vital if decisions are to be made about what the future positioning strategy should be and for appropriate marketing programmes to be developed.

A6 Checklist: Basis for Competing and Brand Positionings

Please read and complete the following checklist.

1. What you should have found out:

Before moving on to the next chapter you should have established the nature of any differential advantages which your business can exploit. If no differential advantages have been found, you must identify areas which have the potential to be developed in the future. Consider what actions must be taken in order to develop current and future differential advantages. You should also have developed one or more positioning maps for your products/ brands. The axes of these maps should be labelled with dimensions which are important to your customers. The KCVs identified earlier in the document will provide an effective starting point. The positions of your products/ brands and those of key competitors (based on the marketplace's perceptions) must be marked on the positioning maps.

If you have not yet collected the necessary information to achieve this, it is vital that you return to this chapter as soon as possible. Marketing programmes must not be formulated until this information is available.

2. Charts which should have been completed:

Make a record of your progress in completing the following charts:

	Status of Analysis		
	Complete	Partly filled	Not complete
A6.1: Identification of differential advantage	❑	❑	❑
A6.2: The positioning map	❑	❑	❑

Be prepared to revisit these charts if/when further relevant information becomes available.

3. Information collected:

The following areas of information are relevant to this chapter. Please indicate your progress in collecting this and other relevant information:

	Information		
	Collected	Collection under way	Not collected
Product/service attributes desired by each segment	❑	❑	❑
Which of the desired product/service attributes are offered by key competitors	❑	❑	❑
Any competitors' DAs	❑	❑	❑
Marketplace perceptions of positioning of the brands/products of the business and competitors	❑	❑	❑
Other.	❑	❑	❑

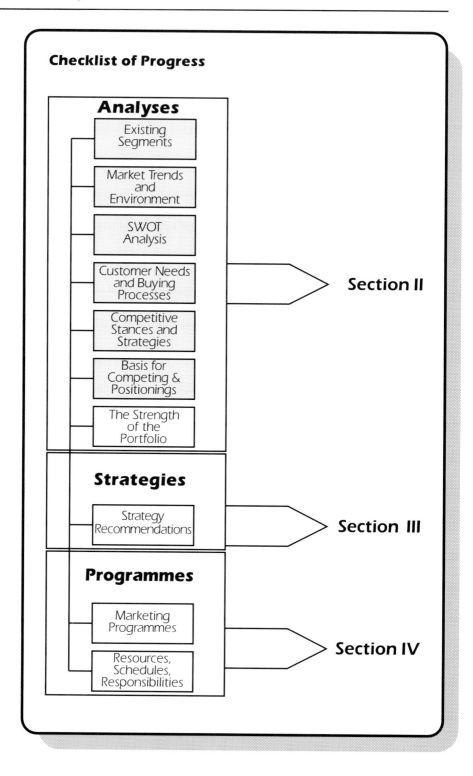

Analyses 7

The Strength of the Portfolio – Future Directions

A7.1 Introduction

Section II has examined the core background analyses which lead to the successful segmentation of a market. The final analysis concerns the health of the existing product portfolio, with the aim of ensuring that the business keeps a balanced portfolio of products.

Portfolio planning tools can be used to weigh up the relative attractiveness of investing in particular businesses and to ensure that an appropriate mix of cash generating and investment requiring areas is maintained by the business. The *Market Attractiveness/Business Position Matrix* (sometimes also referred to as a DPM – Directional Policy Matrix) is one of a range of portfolio planning tools which have been developed to help the business analyse its portfolio.

This chapter uses the Market Attractiveness/Business Position Matrix to build an overview of the business's portfolio of segments. This will allow the current balance of cash-using and cash-generating segments to be assessed and decisions about future resourcing to be made. The analysis also provides a starting point for monitoring the performance of the segments over time.

By the end of this chapter you will have developed one or more matrices which represent the spread of your portfolio of products and segments in terms of market attractiveness and business position. Scores and weightings will have been allocated to a range of factors which your business believes determines market attractiveness and business position in the markets in which you operate. The output from the analysis, represented on the DPM matrices, will then have been analysed.

A7.2 The Directional Policy Matrix Approach to Assessing Business Strength and Market Attractiveness

The aim of the *Market Attractiveness/Business Position Matrix* is to assess the relative attractiveness of investing in particular businesses, so as to determine appropriate strategic planning goals and appropriate funding/manpower. 'Business' can be taken to mean an SBU (strategic business unit), a product group, an individual product or segment. Typically companies set up SBUs on the basis of core product groups, but for the purposes of this exercise it may also be appropriate to use the segment level.

A company reviews the performance of each of its SBUs, products or segments in the context of the company's overall mix of SBUs, segments and product portfolio. The relative 'health'/potential of each SBU (or product) in the context of the overall product portfolio enables the company to decide which SBUs/product groups (or products) to '*build*' (develop further/increase market share of), '*maintain*' (resource to keep the status quo/current market share), '*harvest*' (sell off/pull out of after squeezing the last potential sales), or '*divest*' (drop more or less immediately).

Most managers intuitively know which products are yesterday's 'has-beens' or tomorrow's 'breadwinners'. Managerial impressions, though, are rarely sufficient or robust enough as a basis for such fundamental decision-making. Hence, the development of such analytical techniques by the major consultancies (McKinsey, Boston Consultancy Group) and blue chip companies (General Electric, Shell).

A7.3 Assessing the Market Attractiveness and Business Strength

1. For an SBU, product group or segment, decide which factors are the most appropriate for assessing the *market attractiveness*. Remember that this aspect must be assessed relative to the market as a whole.

2. Separately, repeat for the *business position* (sometimes called the competitive position). This aspect must be assessed relative to the leading/strongest competitor.

These decisions are usually based on the informed judgement of management taking into consideration any relevant research information. Generally, it is best not to exceed five or six factors. For example, when assessing market attractiveness, International Harvester used four: industry sales, product sales, market share and profitability (although this model has seldom been seen elsewhere).

3. Once the two lists of factors have been derived for the market attractiveness and business position, decide how important each of the factors is and allocate an appropriate *weighting*. The total weighting should add up to 100 for each list. For example, when considering

market attractiveness, market size may be considered a particularly important factor and be allocated a weighting of 50.

4. Next, give a *score* to each factor which reflects how the particular market/SBU/product group/segment under consideration shapes up relative to other markets/segments. One way to do this is to make 0.0 = low/poor, 0.5 = medium/average, and 1.0 = high/good. Keep the scoring simple (e.g.: 0, 0.5 and 1).

5. Multiply the weighting by the score to give a *ranking* for each factor. The *sum* of the rankings for each market/SBU/product group/segment analysed should then be calculated.

6. Repeat the process for other SBUs/product groups/segments/products (depending on the chosen level of analysis).

7. Enter each SBU/product group/segment position on the matrix using a circle. The diameter of the circle usually reflects the sales volume of the SBU/segment. Alternatively the circle's diameter can refer to the market size. Whichever is chosen, remain consistent throughout the analysis. If market size is used an area of the circle can be shaded to show the market share of the SBU/product group/segment (as in Figure A7.1).

A7.4 Worked Example

A7.4.1 Market Attractiveness

Factor	Score	Weighting	Ranking
Market size	0.5	25	12.5
Volume growth (units)	0.0	10	0.0
Level of competition	1.0	40	40.0
Technology	1.0	25	25.0
		100	77.5

A7.4.2 Business Position/Competitive Position

Factor	Score	Weighting	Ranking
Product technology			
– quality	1.0	30	30.0
– new technology	0.5	10	5.0
Marketing			
– sales	0.5	20	10.0
– service back-up	1.0	15	15.0
Manufacturing			
– efficiency	0.0	10	0.0
– distribution	0.5	15	7.5
		100	67.5

A7.5 Interpreting the DPM

Figure A7.1 shows an example of a completed matrix and Figure A7.2 the outline strategies to follow.

In general those SBUs/segments/products appearing in the top left of the chart can be deemed as the 'star' products or performers.

Those SBUs/products/segments (depending on the selected level of analysis) which appear in the bottom left of the chart, typically will be the 'cash cows' for the company (those products/SBUs on which the company depends for the bulk of its income/cash generation).

SBUs/segments/products floating around in the centre and top right of the chart tend to be those for which the future is uncertain (in other words over which there is a question mark). For these SBUs/segments/products a decision must be made on whether to cut losses and cease production or to put full marketing/distributor resources behind a major push.

SBUs/segments/products which are located in the bottom right of the chart are the real 'dogs' in the portfolio, with very little potential and probably already making losses. These 'dog' products should be dropped immediately or in the very near future.

A7.6 Levels of Analysis

Commonly, companies tend to undertake this type of analysis first at the product group level, then by pulling together all product groups, for the company as a whole, segment by segment. The analysis can, however, be focused on many levels, such as company-wide for all individual products, for certain product groups/SBUs, for individual products, for specific market segments, separate countries, certain dealer types, or for any permutation. In this instance, you may want to start by looking at the product level and then move on to consider the segment level.

Clearly, though, the concept is intended to look at a company's overall performance and too narrow a focus may detract from the technique's worth. The 'common' approach is for the Marketing Director to focus on the SBU level for all segments, with individual Marketing Managers examining the portfolio at the product level.

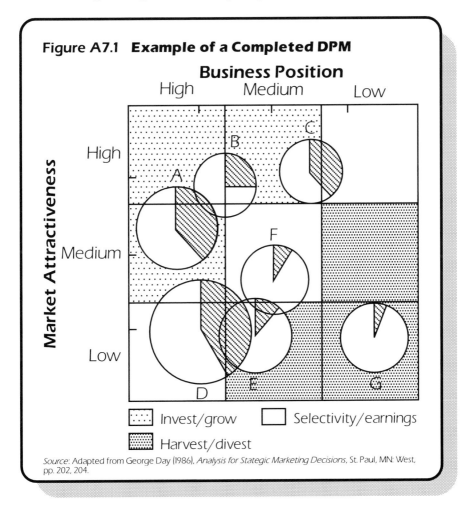

Figure A7.1 Example of a Completed DPM

Source: Adapted from George Day (1986), *Analysis for Stategic Marketing Decisions*, St. Paul, MN: West, pp. 202, 204.

Figure A7.2 Strategy Implications from DPM Positions

	Strong	Medium	Weak
High	**Protect Position** ▪ invest to grow at maximum digestible rate ▪ concentrate effort on maintaining strength	**Invest to Build** ▪ challenge for leadership ▪ build selectively on strengths ▪ reinforce vulnerable areas	**Build Selectively** ▪ specialise around limited strengths ▪ seek ways to overcome weaknesses ▪ withdraw if indications of sustainable growth are lacking
Medium	**Build Selectively** ▪ invest heavily in most attractive segments ▪ build up ability to counter competition ▪ emphasise profitability by raising productivity	**Selectivity/Manage for Earnings** ▪ protect existing programme ▪ concentrate investments in segments where profitability is good and risk is relatively low	**Limited Expansion or Harvest** ▪ look for ways to expand without high risk; otherwise, minimise investment and rationalise operations
Low	**Protect and Refocus** ▪ manage for current earnings ▪ concentrate on attractive segments ▪ defend strengths	**Manage for Earnings** ▪ protect position in most profitable segments ▪ upgrade product line ▪ minimise investment	**Divest** ▪ sell at time that will maximise cash value ▪ cut fixed costs and avoid investment meanwhile

Market Attractiveness (vertical axis) — Business Position (horizontal axis)

Source: Adapted from George Day (1986), *Analysis for Strategic Marketing Decisions*, St Paul, MN: West, pp. 202, 204.

A7.7 Recording The Portfolio Analysis

The factors which make a market attractive need to be determined, scored, weighted and ranked, as in the example above. The same goes for the factors which the company feels affect its business position. Chart A7.1 presents a grid for pulling this information together. Chart A7.2 provides a proforma for the resulting matrices.

Once the relevant matrices have been developed, use Figure A7.2 to assess the positions of the segments which have been plotted. Sometimes managers are surprised or concerned by the position of a particular segment. If this is the case check back that you are happy about the variables, weights and scores which have been used to generate the matrix. Next, consider the implications of the portfolio balance which has been illustrated. Fill in the implications section of Chart A7.2 by identifying segments for investment, defending, managing for earnings, divesting and so on.

Chart A7.1 Information Required for the DPM Analysis

Market Attractiveness			
Factors	**Score**	**Weighting**	**Ranking**

Business/Competitive Position			
Factors	**Score**	**Weighting**	**Ranking**

Actions:
- Select the most important factors. Complete the columns.
- This information now needs to be plotted on Chart A7.2, as in Figure A7.1.

Chart A7.2 **The DPM**

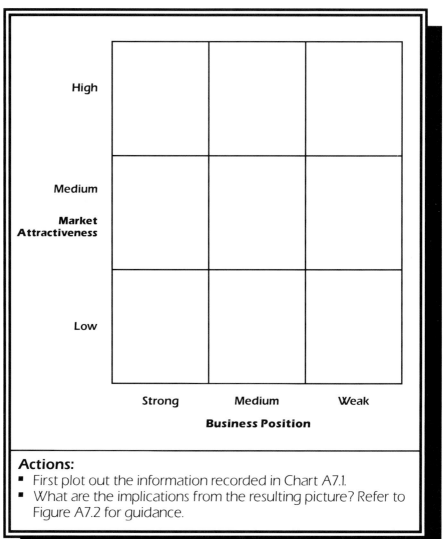

Actions:
- First plot out the information recorded in Chart A7.1.
- What are the implications from the resulting picture? Refer to Figure A7.2 for guidance.

The Market Attractiveness/Business Position matrix provides a useful starting point for comparing the progress of segments over time. It is helpful to regenerate the matrices in 6 and 12 months' time, so that any movement or change in size of the segments can be monitored. One word of caution – to be comparable, matrices generated at different points in time *must* use the same variables and variable weightings. Companies sometimes fall into the trap of changing the criteria, with meaningless results. This is equivalent to measuring your height in centimetres one day and in inches the next, but not allowing for the difference in measures!

A7.8 Summary

The DPM can be used to assess the health of the business in terms of the balance of product groups or segments. By reviewing the performance of each SBU, product or segment, within the context of the business's overall portfolio, decisions can be made about the most appropriate areas in which to invest. Cash-draining areas can also be identified so that, if necessary, a divestment strategy can be determined. The DPM is useful in determining the health of the current portfolio as well as in longer-term planning.

A7 Checklist: The Strength of the Portfolio

Please read and complete the following checklist.

1. What you should have found out:

Before moving on to the next chapter you should have developed a Directional Policy Matrix(s) for your product groups and/or segments. This will have involved deciding which factors are the most appropriate for assessing *market attractiveness* and *business position* in your industry. You will also have determined relevant weightings and scores for each factor, which you believe reflects a) how your business shapes up relative to competitors and b) the relative attractiveness of the industry. Once the DPMs have been plotted, you will have considered the implications in terms of possible future strategies.

If you have not yet collected the necessary information to achieve this, it is vital that you return to this chapter as soon as possible.

2. Charts which should have been completed:

Make a record of your progress in completing the following charts:

	Status of Analysis		
	Complete	Partly filled	Not complete
A7.1: Information required for the DPM analysis	☐	☐	☐
A7.2: The Directional Policy Matrix and implications	☐	☐	☐

Be prepared to revisit these charts if/when further relevant information becomes available.

3. Information collected:

The following areas of information are relevant to this chapter. Please indicate your progress in collecting this and other relevant information. Blank space has been included to allow you to name the factors which you have identified when determining market attractiveness and business position:

	Information		
	Collected	Collection under way	Not collected
Market attractiveness factors: e.g.: market share	❏ ❏ ❏ ❏ ❏	❏ ❏ ❏ ❏ ❏	❏ ❏ ❏ ❏ ❏
Business position factors:	❏ ❏ ❏ ❏	❏ ❏ ❏ ❏	❏ ❏ ❏ ❏
Other.	❏	❏	❏

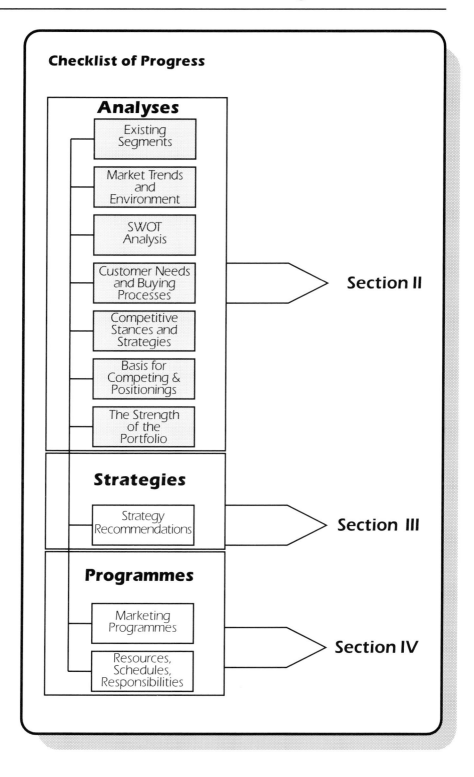

Checklist of Progress

Analyses

- Existing Segments
- Market Trends and Environment
- SWOT Analysis
- Customer Needs and Buying Processes
- Competitive Stances and Strategies
- Basis for Competing & Positionings
- The Strength of the Portfolio

Section II

Strategies

- Strategy Recommendations

Section III

Programmes

- Marketing Programmes
- Resources, Schedules, Responsibilities

Section IV

Section III

Strategy

The analyses described in chapter A4 (Customers) play a vital role in identifying segments and revising existing customer groupings. The remaining analyses help determine other strategic issues such as which segments to prioritise and how to position the business's products within targeted segments vis-à-vis competitors' offerings. Section III of this book addresses these strategic issues: the steps entailed in revising customer groupings and defining market segments; the issues to consider when establishing targets; and, the determination of desired brand positioning in the key segments.

Carrying out the analyses in Section II required a careful process of research and information gathering. This section demands careful consideration of all available information, some debate and the commitment to allow the updated marketing intelligence to input into the business's decision-making. Without the analyses outlined in Section II, it is simply not possible to progress with Section III.

By the end of this section you should realise why the initial definition of customer groups employed by the business will need to evolve and change. The importance of understanding customers' needs (KCVs), buying processes, influencing factors and their perceptions of rival brands will be demonstrated. Clear step-by-step instructions will be presented explaining how to use the information from the analyses to revise segment groupings, re-examine the list of priority target markets, and determine how you want the business's products to be perceived – positioned – in each target segment. Help is also available in assessing newly identified segments currently not served by the business. The section concludes with a clear strategy summary statement and a discussion of the major problems to overcome if the strategy is to be feasible. By working through this section and completing the accompanying charts, you will determine your business's target market strategy.

Section III Contents
Chapter S1: Strategy Recommendations

S1

Strategy Recommendations

S1.1 Introduction

The background analyses (chapter A1) have highlighted the strengths and weaknesses implicit in the current view of core target markets, and the need to update key customer targets. The additional analyses (chapters A2 to A7) have brought together a depth of information relating to the market and its current characteristics: customer needs and expectations; general market trends and impacting aspects of the external marketing environment; competitive positions and competitors' strengths; the business's basis for competing and differential advantage; brand or product positionings; strengths, weaknesses, opportunities and threats; and, the balance of the existing product portfolio.

In the light of this information strategy decisions have now to be made. It is likely that existing strategies will be altered. This chapter divides into three main parts:

- How to group together customers with 'similar' needs and buying behaviour.
- Which groups of customers to target and which to prioritise.
- How to position the business's offerings within the selected segment(s).

S1.2 Segmenting Customer Groups

S1.2.1 Grouping Customers with Similar Needs

The approach adopted in this book is pragmatic: the starting point is how the business currently defines its customer groups rather than a blank sheet of paper on which each individual customer can be appraised and allocated to totally novel segments. In most businesses, to start afresh would be unmanageable and hotly contested by senior colleagues, sales personnel, distributors and often suppliers. The more pragmatic approach, however, can still lead to the formation of productive market segments in the sense that customer groups are constructed on the basis of customers' needs and buying behaviour.

In view of the trends in the marketplace and the characteristics identified as to which customers bring the most benefit, how *they* buy, and what factors influence *their* decisions, the question is whether customers can be grouped differently than described originally in Chart A1.1? The answer, to a degree, is probably 'yes'. For most businesses, there will be benefits but also certain flaws in the existing grouping employed.

It should now be possible to determine which aspects from the improved understanding of these customers can be used as the basis for grouping customers for sales and marketing purposes.

There is a range of possible factors to consider. As explained in chapter 2 of Section I, these variables will differ for business-to-business and consumer markets.

1 *Business-to-business markets*

- Geographic location
- Type/size
- Product usage
- Size and frequency of orders
- Supplier loyalty/switching
- Delivery requirements
- Trade category
- Business sector

2 *Consumer markets*

- Location
- Demographics
- Brand loyalty
- Product usage
- Benefits sought
- Brand perceptions
- Attitudes
- Socio-economic characteristics
- Motivation
- Lifestyle
- Purchase behaviour
- Purchase occasion
- Consumption behaviour

There are no fixed right or wrong answers to this part of the process. It is important, though, for managers to tune in to the particular nuances of their markets. For example, there may be customers who are more responsive to or aware of external trends than others, such as those who are more concerned about the ecological impact of product disposal or manufacturing processes. Another possibility may be to consider those whose business or income fluctuates more dramatically in line with general economic patterns. Alternatively, there may be customers whose business or markets, or lifestyles are more obviously affected by political or regulatory controls.

At this juncture, it is necessary to build up a comprehensive picture on which to base segmentation decisions. Addressing a series of wide-ranging questions, which relate to the customers and their behaviour, is usually a productive way to proceed.

How are customers affected by the marketing environment? Does such behaviour cause the business to group several customers together? How may these factors affect how the customers behave when making a purchase?

What is the typical buying process undertaken by each type of customer (see Chart A4.1)? What are the influences on this buying process? How brand/manufacturer loyal are customers? Inevitably there will be traits here which apply to several customers, often cutting across the commonly adopted segmentation parameters of customer size, type, location and product use in industrial markets, or socio-economics, lifestyles and demographics in consumer markets.

It is vital to take stock of these issues, *prior* to deciding on customer targets and to determining sales and marketing programmes. The outcome from the segmentation study must be groupings of customers based on 'similar' needs and buying behaviour. It is likely that the existing view of how customers are grouped will change as a result of analysing customers' buying behaviour and needs (KCVs).

The following criteria are the basis for the examination of the customer base and regrouping or reclassifying of customers into market segments.

- Which customer needs (KCVs) help to group customers with 'similar' needs together?
- Which aspects of the marketing environment can affect customers differently and so input to these grouping criteria?
- What are the customers' buying processes, decision-making criteria and levels of brand loyalty?

Once the new, larger list of criteria to consider is determined, it is possible to allocate individual customers into segments of 'similar' customers either intuitively – by judgement – or statistically.

In most cases new segments will be identified. Some of the existing, broadly defined customer groups will be further sub-divided. Based on the analyses outlined in Section II of this book, the nature of the business's customer groupings will change. In addition, the output from the marketing analyses undertaken in Section II will present innumerable issues to be addressed in the redefinition of core target markets.

S1.2.2 Step-by-Step Guide to Re-segmenting

Section II of this book detailed the marketing analyses required for the segmentation process. Once these analyses are complete, the following steps need to be undertaken in order to re-examine how customers should be grouped into market segments. The charts listed have been featured in the analyses chapters.

1. List the existing segments. These typically will be at a broad level (Chart A1.1).

2. On Chart A1.2, list the importance to the business of these segments for the past five or ten years and include the forecast for next year. (See Chart A1.2.) In other words, rank the segments for each year. Make sure the current year's ranking is 'typical'. If it is typical, use the current year's situation for the rest of this analysis. If there is an unusual blip – peak or trough – re-think the ranking.

3. Using sales and contribution data, plot out an ABC Sales: Contribution graph (see Chart A1.3) for the segments listed at (1). Segments to the top right of this chart require the most consideration as they present the best rewards. If there are many segments to consider as part of this study, commence with those to the top right of the ABC sales: contribution chart.

4. It is likely that the broad definitions of the existing segments can be now further refined into sub-segments. For example, an agro-chemicals manufacturer had segments in Latin America based on crops grown by the farmers: a soya segment, maize, rice and so on. Each was found to contain several distinct sub-groups of farmers, with different KCVs and buying processes. The original soya sector was deemed to be in fact five sub-groups.

Think about whether any of the business's original broad segments need to be so sub-divided. If they can, make appropriate sub-divisions to the broad segments, but only where there is obvious reason for doing so.

[Note: on the KCV form (Chart A1.1) – see (6) below – there must be apparent differences between these newly listed sub-groups – they should be discrete, otherwise they should *not* be listed as separate groups! One business sub-divided a sector into five segments only to discover that while three of them had different labels and types of customers, they shared identical KCVs and buyer processes. These three were really one segment, so that the original sector should have been split into three segments and not five].

5. Continue the rest of this analysis (steps 6 to 10) for the newly defined sub-segment/sub-group level.

6. Complete a KCV form (see Chart A1.1 for an explanation) for each sub-segment listed. Remember that the KCVs must be those deemed important *by customers*, not just by the business's managers. In the list of KCVs per segment, rank the KCVs in order of importance.

Note that if the KCVs for any sub-segment or customer group cannot be generalised, the apparent segment is clearly not homogeneous and it would be incorrect to treat this group of customers as being similar. In reality, there may well be two or more sub-groups incorrectly grouped together and these should be sub-divided according to their KCVs.

7. For each sub-segment, complete Chart A4.1 (The Buying Process). This covers for each segment the buying process, influences on each step in this process, KCVs, and a description of each customer type.

If the buying process differs dramatically for first-time buyers and regular, repeat buyers, produce two forms.

As with KCVs, if the buying process cannot easily be generalised across the customers allocated to a particular segment or customer group, it is likely that customers have been incorrectly grouped together. They will need to be sub-divided into sub-groups according to their KCVs and buying processes.

8. For the final list of segments and sub-groups, complete a differential advantage/competitive positions form (Chart A5.1).

All of the basic information required to regroup customers into segments is now to hand. A segment contains customers with common needs (KCVs), buying processes and similar influences, and competitors' products are similar.

It might be that the original customer grouping employed by the business and described in Chart A1.1 is robust and stands up after re-examining KCVs and buying processes. It is likely, however, that some changes will be required in the business's definition of segments. Stages 1 to 7 will address any need for the sub-division of existing groups. The result may be an increased number of customer groups. The important question is now whether any of these can be aggregated together. The next step deals with this issue.

9. Take the three crucial analyses:

- KCVs (Chart A1.1)
- Buying Process (Chart A4.1)
- Differential Advantage/Competitive Positions (Chart A5.1)

Where there are common KCVs, buying processes, influences (and competing brands), then these sub-segments logically should be aggregated – probably across customer type (e.g. for the agro-chemicals manufacturer in Latin America, across farmer crop type and across its own product groups) – to form *genuine*, productive market segments. In the case of the agro-chemicals supplier, the business decided that certain farmers should be grouped into a segment on the basis of their overall product requirements, buying worries, dealer needs, geographic location and farm size, irrespective of whether they grew soya, wheat, maize or rice.

10. Identify these common threads where sub-groups share KCVs and buying processes, and regroup any sub-segments together. Note, it is likely that only a few will be regrouped. Many of the sub-segments will be sufficiently unique to leave unaltered as separate segments.

Use Chart S1.1 to summarise the changes.

To clarify the role of the additional marketing analyses discussed in Section II of this book, they are required when making decisions about which segments the business should target, as detailed in S1.2.

Chart S1.1 **Summary of Segment Changes**

List of Original Customer Groups From Chart A1.1	Newly Identified Customer Groups/Segments	Explanation: Why are These New Groups/Segments so Defined?
▪	1.	?1.
▪	2.	?2.
▪	3.	?3.
▪	4.	?4.
▪	5.	?5.
▪	6.	?6.
▪	7.	?7.
▪	8.	?8.
▪	9.	?9.
▪	10.	?10.

Actions:
- Use Chart S1.1 to summarise changes to how customer groups (segments) are now defined.
- Explain in column 3 why the new segments are so defined.

S1.2.3 Segmenting Customer Groups: Concluding Remarks

The process just outlined helped a manufacturer of construction equipment to move from customer groups determined by the company's product groups and territorial presence to segments containing customers with similar needs and buying processes. Customers requiring compact equipment had different product and service requirements, with a need for specialised dealerships from customers buying heavy line extractive equipment for quarrying and road building. Each segment required unique marketing programmes. The revised approach brought the company internal economies of scales – four segments to service rather than seven product groups to market to twenty-five countries – with enhanced customer satisfaction and dealer loyalty.

A car manufacturer was able to move away from its view of customer groups as big, medium and small car buyers to carefully defined customer groups, each requiring a unique product mix and supportive marketing programmes. A national supermarket chain had viewed customers as up-market, middle market or price-conscious, in-town or car-borne. While income was important, as was car ownership in terms of out-of-town shopping, there were far more important criteria in terms of customer needs and shopping habits to consider in determining customer groupings and prioritising the company's targets.

Finally, when addressing how to re-segment the business's customer base, remember that it is essential to:

1. Look at how customers are currently grouped. Can they be further sub-divided? Do the customers in each group share similar KCVs and buying processes?

2. Check if once additional customer groups/sub-groups have been identified, are they really different? Are they robust? Do similar KCVs and buying processes hold true for all those customers in each group?

3. Determine if any of the sub-groups can be aggregated together (probably cutting across the business's original view of customer groups) to form market segments. Can sub-groups which exhibit similar KCVs and buying processes be regrouped with each other to form larger, but homogeneous segments?

S1.3 Determining the Targeting Strategy

S1.3.1 Revising Target Segment Selection

By now it should be evident that a whole host of factors has highlighted the need to revise the business's selection of key customer targets and of key target markets. Not just the sales: contribution financial performance analysis. It should also be clear that more than buyer purchase behaviour and general market trends need to impact on the selection of customer targets.

Competitors' positions and strategies; the business's strengths and weaknesses; basis for competing and any differential advantage; the product life cycle and need for a balanced portfolio, are all additional issues which should play a role in determining target market strategy.

S1.3.2 Step-by-Step Guide to Targeting

This section provides a step-by-step guide to making the necessary targeting decisions, utilising the required marketing intelligence.

1. Take completed core analyses as described in Section II of this book:

- differential advantages for the business (if any) per segment (see Chart A6.1);
- brand positionings versus competitors (see Chart A6.2);
- marketing environment trends, identifying any issues particularly pertinent for individual segments (see Chart A2.2);
- sales patterns over time (see Chart A2.1);
- SWOT analyses, emphasising any aspects especially relevant to individual segments (see Chart A3.1); and
- balance of product portfolio (see Chart A7.2).

2. Remember also to take into consideration:

- competitive positions per segment (see Chart A5.1);
- ABC/financial worth assessments per segment (see Chart A1.3); and
- customer needs, buying processes, influences (see Charts A4.1 and 4.2).

It does not require a leap of faith when faced with the output from these analyses to reconsider target market priorities. One petrochemicals business was shocked at its unflattering competitive position outside its European heartland. It radically overhauled its choice of target markets to take account of its realistic potential given the competition's superior position. However, in America it was able to use guerrilla tactics to steal market share from the leading players.

Market trends often dictate future priorities, but if these are not being monitored a company will be reactive and only exit from segments after a sales crisis has occurred. The business may well miss out on exploiting newly emerging opportunities, allowing a more aware competitor to take the edge. Equally, a proper understanding of available resources, internal strengths and weaknesses leads to a realisation of the need to select only the most valuable and potentially lucrative segments as most businesses are not capable or adequately resourced to address all of the markets initially deemed interesting.

Segments with a weak competitive position may be less attractive, while others in which there are perceived differential advantages (DAs) will be more appealing as target priorities, having a strong basis for competing. Segments which are currently important may become less of a priority as a scan of the marketing environment reveals market trends which are unattractive. The internal situation – strengths and weaknesses from the SWOT and the picture from the ABC sales: contribution chart – will force hard decisions given weaknesses and relevant strengths to exploit opportunities, and in budgeting. Much more than existing sales volumes and estimated market sizes must affect the decision of which segments to target.

Superimposing the marketing analyses detailed in Section II and examining the results together should present a more realistic view of genuine marketing opportunities and segments to target than the information given purely by a simplistic SWOT analysis or a review of sales figures. Differential advantage, competitor strengths, brand positionings, market trends, SWOT issues, the balance of the portfolio, sales: contribution status and sales figures must *all* play a role in targeting segments, as well as the business's ability to properly service targeted customers' needs and buying requirements.

It is important to point out that the analyses conducted so far give a complete picture of the *existing* sectors or segments of operation. They do *not* examine any other segments in the marketplace in which the business currently is not active. The following section gives guidance when reviewing segments which are new to the business.

S1.3.3 Targeting Segments New to The Business

This section considers other segments in the market not currently addressed by the business. For example, these may be segments in which competitors are active or which are not adequately served by any player.

1. Complete core analyses forms as detailed in Section II of this book for each of the identified segments new to the business:

- KCVs (see Chart A1.1);
- buying process/influences (see Chart A4.1);
- marketing environment/trends (see Chart A2.2);
- competitive positions/differential advantage (see Chart A5.1);
- brand positionings along key KCV attributes (see Chart A6.2).

2. Consider the attractiveness to the business of these new segments in the light of these analyses.

- Trends/value
- Potential differential advantage for the business; capabilities.
It is likely that not all of the new segments will appear attractive.

3. Consider the degree to which these other segments are 'unique'. Given their KCVs, customer needs, buying processes, can any of these segments be merged with any of the major segments in which the business is already active?

If newly identified customers could be merged with relevant existing segments, there would be distribution, sales and marketing economies as new products for these segments are introduced. Most new groups will not be suitable to merge, but it is possible that a few could prove to be appropriate.

S1.3.4 Target Markets: Concluding Remarks

The output from sections S1.3.2 (Guide to Targeting) and S1.3.3 (Targeting Segments New to the Business) needs to be combined so that decisions can be made about segment selection and prioritisation. Chart S1.2 provides a simple format for summarising target markets in order of priority for the business. This appraisal will need to consider which segments are most attractive to the business as discussed in S1.3.2. Make sure it also identifies any segments which must be included in the priority list as a defence for the business's overall position and activities in related segments.

Chart S1.2 **Target Segment Selection Summary**

Segment 1: _____ _Healthy eating_ _____
Segment Profile Description: _30+ food aware, health-conscious, discerning buyers._
Why is this segment important? _____
_____ _Trend for more health-conscious eating, growing market._ _____
_____

Segment 2: _____ _Kiddies' Corner_ _____
Segment Profile Description: _____ _Children – young. Jun Sector._ _____
Why is this segment important? _____
_____ _Volume. Profitability. Future adult consumers._ _____
_____ _Already important and must be defended._ _____

Segment 3: _____ _Family_ _____
Segment Profile Description: _____ _General household, Traditional cereals._ _____
Why is this segment important? _____
_____ _Dormant but signs of growth._ _____
_____ _Business must be active here to defend other segments._ _____

Segment 4: _____
Segment Profile Description: _____
Why is this segment important? _____
_____
_____

Segment 5: _____
Segment Profile Description: _____
Why is this segment important? _____
_____
_____

Segment 6: _____
Segment Profile Description: _____
Why is this segment important? _____
_____
_____

Segment 7: _____
Segment Profile Description: _____
Why is this segment important? _____
_____
_____

Segment 8: _____
Segment Profile Description: _____
Why is this segment important? _____
_____
_____

Action:
- List newly determined segments in rank order of importance.

S1.4 Required Positioning

S1.4.1 Developing Positioning/Perceptual Maps

The target segments have now been determined and priorities established. The next step is to determine the required product or brand positioning in each targeted segment. With the aid of a positioning perceptual map (see Figure A6.2), this involves explaining for each target segment the required positioning vis-à-vis the key competitors. The Key Customer Values (KCVs) identified in Charts A1.1 and A4.1 should form the axes for these positioning maps. It may be appropriate to construct more than one perceptual map for segments in which more than two KCVs are deemed to be high priority to customers. Remember, these dimensions must be seen as important by the customers rather than just by the business's own executives.

Understanding relative brand positionings is a fundamental step in the determination of strategy. All too often companies base far reaching decisions on hastily prepared and ill-thought out positioning maps. The following guidelines will help to ensure such difficulties do not occur here.

- Make sure the maps are based on customers' identified needs.
- Take into account competitors' positionings and their ability to deliver to these customer needs.
- Whenever possible use feedback from customers to ensure objectivity.
- Maximise any identified differential advantage (DA) held by the business by feeding the information into sales and marketing programmes.
- Check that the suggested positioning recommendations are reasonable, especially if major shifts in customers' perceptions are desired.

Using Chart S1.3 indicate the existing positionings for the business and its rivals' brands (as in Chart A6.2), and mark the desired brand position for the business. This should be realistic given existing customer perceptions and needs to be undertaken for each segment targeted.

Chart S1.3 Desired Brand Positioning

Segment: _____

High

Variable:
_____

Low

Low   Variable: _____   High

Statement of Desired Positioning:

Actions:
- Copy existing brand positionings from Chart A6.2.
- Add the desired positioning for the business's brands in this segment. Be realistic!
- Repeat for each target segment.

S1.4.2 Required Positioning: Concluding Remarks

It is not unusual for management consultants assisting with marketing planning or target marketing, in a particular business, to be faced with unrealistic and over-optimistic positioning maps. Such businesses would do well to remember that:

a) customer satisfaction is all-important,

b) customers' opinions are more important than those of the business's own managers, and

c) customers' views take time to change.

Customers base their purchase decisions on their brand or product perceptions: the business's brands versus rivals' offerings in the context of key customer needs (KCVs). Establishing a clear positioning is important, but this requires deliberate communications programmes with realistic objectives.

One of the principal aims of the eventual marketing programmes, as discussed next in Section IV, must be to offer products and services which deliver this desired product positioning to the targeted customers, with programmes which communicate the proposition to these target customers.

S1.5 Strategy Recommendations: Putting Segmentation, Targeting and Positioning Together

At this stage it is helpful to take stock of progress to date. A number of questions should be posed. In the light of the core analyses so far undertaken, which are the core markets to target? Why these? What will be the likely sales achieved by the business in each segment? What are the most important customer needs (KCVs) in each segment for the business to satisfy? Where lies the market opportunity in each segment? Therefore, what are the main objectives to be addressed in the segments targeted? To achieve the objectives, sales targets and customer satisfaction, what is the required brand positioning in each segment? Who are the principal rivals and what is the most pressing competitive threat? Is there any differential advantage (DA) to help the business combat this threat? What problems need to be overcome if the target market strategy is to succeed? Are there any capital implications stemming from the determined strategy? This is a long list of important questions, each of which should by now have been considered. Each must be addressed before the strategy can be actioned.

Chart S1.4 presents a summary format for the strategy recommendations and issues.

Chart S1.4 **Target Market Strategy Summary Statement**

Core Target Segments						
Segment	1:	2:	3:	4:	5:	6:
Principal Reason for Segment Being Target Priority	•	•	•	•	•	•
Likely Sales Current Year	-	-	-	-	-	-
Likely Sales Next Year	-	-	-	-	-	-
Likely Sales in Two Years	-	-	-	-	-	-
KCVs per Segment	1 2 3 4	1 2 3 4	1 2 3 4	1 2 3 4	1 2 3 4	1 2 3 4
Major Market Opportunity	•	•	•	•	•	•
Principal Marketing Objective	•	•	•	•	•	•
Required Brand Positioning	•	•	•	•	•	•
Main Two Competitors	1 2	1 2	1 2	1 2	1 2	1 2
Main Competitive Threat	•	•	•	•	•	•
Differential Advantage (DA) Held (if any)	-	-	-	-	-	-
Key Problems to Overcome	- -	- -	- -	- -	- -	- -
Capital Implications from Strategy	•	•	•	•	•	•

• It is important to complete Chart S1.4 comprehensively: it is the overall statement of target market strategy and drives the marketing programmes.

The problems to overcome in Chart S1.5 must be tackled. If they are not, the successful implementation of the stated target market strategy is unlikely. Many of these problems may be politically sensitive, resource-demanding and require time to address. It is particularly important, therefore, to state these problems clearly and for 'ownership' of tackling them to be allocated to individual managers. These problems will not be solved by inertia! Chart S1.5. is designed to help overcome these implementation difficulties.

Chart S1.5 Tackling the Core Problems

E.g.: Innovative packaging material

The Core Problems to Overcome

Problem to Overcome	Segment/ Segments	Action Required	Who to Assess Problem	When to Assess	Cost Implication
▪ Sales force inertia		Senior management involvement. Training.			
▪ Lack of customer understanding		Education.			
▪ Promotional budgets high		Canvassing of Board.			
▪					
▪					
▪					

Actions:
- Summarise the problems to overcome identified in Chart S1.4.
- Use Chart S1.5 to ensure these problems are tackled.

S1.6 Summary

This chapter has encouraged you to use the marketing intelligence provided by the analyses detailed in Section II to:

a) revise the business's groupings of customers into market segments;

b) update the business's view as to which are the most important target markets; and

c) determine a realistic positioning strategy versus rivals for the business's products in each segment.

Help is also offered for assessing segments new to the business, in which the business has not previously been active and has not offered any products. By the end of this section the key strategic issues should have been addressed and a clear target market strategy determined. These issues are pulled together in the Target Market Strategy Summary Statement displayed in Chart S1.4. The most significant problems standing in the way of this strategy will have been highlighted.

The resulting marketing strategy recommendations should be different from those being followed by the business prior to this exercise. If they are not, either the core marketing analyses described in Section II have not been conducted thoroughly and with objectivity, or the output from these analyses has not been properly taken into account. The next section of this book addresses the action programmes required to implement the target market strategy determined in this section. Until Chart S1.4 has been sensibly and honestly filled in, there is little point continuing into Section IV.

S1 Checklist: Strategy Recommendations

Please read and complete the following checklist.

1. What you should have determined:

Before moving on to the next section of this book, the results from the core marketing analyses outlined previously in Section II *must* lead to a revision of the business's target market strategy. The initial definition of customer groups will be revised to allow the identification of market segments. Segments entirely new to the business may be considered. Those segments determined must be prioritised as targets for the business. For each segment on the priority target list, the business must decide on its brand/product positioning strategy vis-à-vis competitors. There will be problems facing such a strategy: these must be addressed.

You cannot complete the segmentation process – by considering marketing programmes for implementation in Section IV – until the recommended target market strategy outlined in this Section has been painstakingly considered and revised.

2. Charts which should have been completed:

Make a record of your progress in completing the following charts:

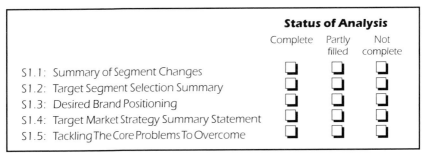

	Status of Analysis		
	Complete	Partly filled	Not complete
S1.1: Summary of Segment Changes	☐	☐	☐
S1.2: Target Segment Selection Summary	☐	☐	☐
S1.3: Desired Brand Positioning	☐	☐	☐
S1.4: Target Market Strategy Summary Statement	☐	☐	☐
S1.5: Tackling The Core Problems To Overcome	☐	☐	☐

Progress cannot continue unless these charts are now completed.

3. Information required:

The following areas of information are required for work in this Section.

	Information Collected
For segmentation;	
List of existing customer groups, A1.1	☐
Importance of existing customer groups, A1.2	☐
ABC sales: contribution analysis, A1.3	☐
Competitive positions, A5.1	☐
but most significantly,	
Customer needs and buyer behaviour, A4.1	☐
For targeting:	
Sales patterns, A2.1	☐
ABC sales: contribution analysis, A1.3	☐
Marketing environment trends, A2.2	☐
SWOT issues, A3.1	☐
Balance of the portfolio, A7.2	☐
Competitive positions, A5.1	☐
Differential advantages (DAs), A6.1	☐
Brand positionings, A6.2	☐
Customer needs and behaviour, A4.1	☐

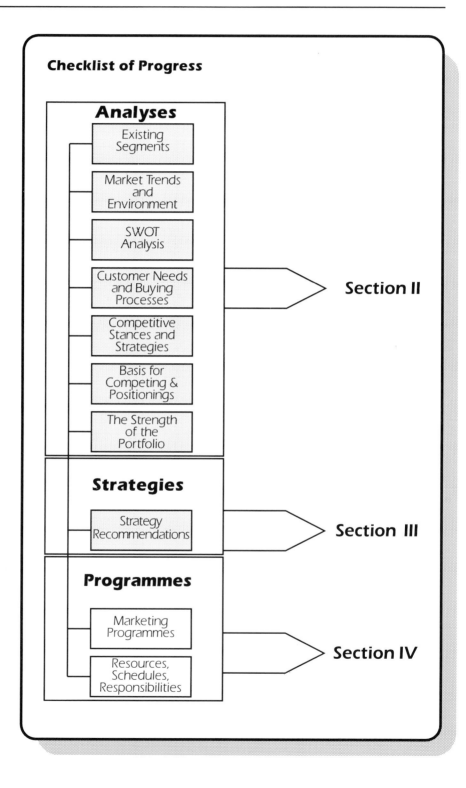

Section IV

Programmes for Implementation

Introduction

The process presented in this book has been designed to ensure that core marketing analyses are undertaken and that strategic decisions are made with thought and due concern to the updated marketing intelligence. These analyses and the revised target market priorities will only improve the business's situation if marketing programmes are put in place which implement the desired strategy. This section of the book is designed to formulate the required marketing actions and to schedule them into well structured programmes for implementation.

There are various aspects to putting together implementation programmes. First and foremost, each target market requires its own, bespoke *marketing mix*: product mix, pricing, channels and distribution, promotional campaigns and people/customer service. There may well be some overlaps between segments, bringing associated economies of scale, but in general the differing KCVs and competitive situation will necessitate each segment having its own set of marketing activities. The marketing mix issues must be controlled: personnel should be assigned to action these marketing recommendations, there need to be clear schedules, and budgets must be calculated and allocated.

It is possible that not all designated activity will be feasible immediately. There will be on-going development required, particularly in new products, marketing research and altering brand perceptions. The specified marketing programmes must also take account of these on-going needs, and allocate personnel responsible for progressing these actions. There may well be knock-on ramifications for other parts of the business (e.g. production/engineering, sister companies, agencies, personnel and treasury departments). These ramifications must be raised if implementation of the desired marketing programmes is to occur. Failure to address these issues will prevent the recommended target market strategy outlined in the previous section being achieved.

Section IV Contents

Marketing Programmes

P1.1 Introduction

In order to achieve the strategy recommendations (Section III), it is necessary to develop appropriate marketing programmes. This section presents the actions required to address the targeted segments and is crucial for the successful implementation of the recommended target market strategy. These marketing programmes must be specific, hard hitting, meaningful and capable of implementation given available resources. Above all, the programmes must reflect the analyses undertaken and the strategy recommendations made.

There is no point conducting the analyses which identify issues the company needs to address through its strategy, if the sales and marketing activities in the business remain the same. Simply reinstating existing marketing programmes will not move the company on, nor equip it for forthcoming encounters with its competitors.

By the end of this chapter you will have developed marketing programmes for *each* segment targeted which reflect customer needs and expectations, desired brand positioning and the business's competitive position. These marketing programmes will cover all elements of the marketing mix: products, pricing, place (distribution), promotion and people/customer service.

P1.2 Developing Programmes

Throughout the development of marketing programmes it is necessary to stress a number of core issues: key customer values/needs (the KCVs), competitive threats, any differential advantage over rivals and the required brand positioning (see Chart P1.1). To lose sight of these issues will render the analyses and recommended strategies redundant as the final marketing actions will not reflect the strategic needs of the business. After all, the marketing programmes must be developed with the intention for each target segment of satisfying customers' needs, matching or beating competitors' moves, emphasising any strengths or differential advantages, while achieving the desired brand positioning.

When formulating marketing programmes, an awareness of existing marketing programmes is necessary. It is highly likely that many

Chart P1.1 **Summary by Segment of KCVs and DAs**
E.g.: Crystal glassware/ceramics

	Segment 1: Business Gifts – Specials	Segment 2: Business Gifts – Suppliers	Segment 3: etc.	Segment 4:	Segment 5:	Segment 6:
Summary of KCVs	• Variety • Gift image • Reputation of supplier • Value	• Gift image • Bulk deals • Rapid lead times • Value				
Main Competitive Threat to the Business	• Diversity of competitors • Competitor X's new pricing	• Price competition • Low brand awareness • No. of competitors				
Any DA Held by the Business? What?	Brand image in crystal only	None				
Desired positioning	The 'Cartier' of the market	Reliable and good value – the Ford Escort of this market				

of these activities will continue. However, given the analyses so far undertaken and the revised target segment strategy determined, a certain degree of revision of existing programmes is inevitable.

There are five fundamental areas to be addressed: product, pricing, distribution (channels to market), promotion and people/service – the marketing mix elements.

P1.3 **The Marketing Mix**

In order to understand areas of weakness, it is important to be aware of current *perceptions* in the target markets for brand awareness; product image; product quality; after sales support and dealer/distributor coverage; value of product/deliverable; product performance and product safety, versus the main competitors. Chart P1.2 should be used to summarise the necessary details and explain where improvements are needed.

Chart P1.2 **Customer Perceptions Versus Leading Rivals**

	Current Perceptions for Segment: *Business Gifts – Special*				
	Positive		Neutral	Negative	
	++	+	+/−	−	−−
Brand Awareness	*1*	*2B*			
Product Image	*1*	*2B*			
Product Quality		*1B2*			
After Sales Support			*1B2*		
Value of Deliverable		*12*	*B*		
Product Performance		*1*	*B2*		
Product Safety					
Dealer Coverage	*1*	*2*	*B*		
Other: *Range*		*1B*	*2*		
Other: *Lead Times*		*12*	*B*		

Actions:
- Produce one form per targeted segment.
- First enter the business's rating: ++, +, +/−, − or −−. NB: ++ = very positive/ good; +/− = neutral; −− = highly negative/very poor.
- Second enter the ratings for the two leading rivals in the segment.
- Use a coding to mark companies on the chart: B = *The Business*; 1 = main rival; 2 = second main rival. Competitor 1 is: *WATERFORD* Competitor 2 is: *ROYAL DOULTON*.

P1.3.1 The '5Ps' of the Marketing Mix

The Marketing Mix is the tool kit of any marketing department, consisting of the '5 Ps': Product (actual good or a service), Pricing, Place (Distribution/Channels to Market), Promotion and People. Traditionally, marketing texts have referred to the '4Ps', but it is now acknowledged there is a need to highlight specifically people/customer service issues. Each target market segment requires a bespoke marketing mix or set of marketing programmes.

1. *Product*: actions for product additions, modifications, deletions, design, positioning, branding;

2. *Price*: pricing/payment policies to be followed for each product group in each segment;

3. *Place*: policies for distribution channels and service levels;

4. *Promotion*: policies for communicating with customers, dealers/distributors and the sales force through advertising, sales promotion, public relations and publicity, exhibitions/trade shows, direct mail, sponsorship and with personal selling/the sales force; and

5. *People*: individuals concerned with delivering aspects of the service or product – and of the sales and marketing programmes – to customers and those concerned with handling sales and service.

See illustrative caselet below.

Background caselet: Crystal Clear Ltd

Note: this material is included to give background to the brief examples included in each of the charts presented in this chapter. This is a fictitious company and should not be confused with any real organisation. This material is for illustrative purposes only.

Founded at the turn of the century, Crystal Clear Ltd is now one of the world's major manufacturers of fine leaded crystal. From its south-west of England base the company has spread its distribution coverage throughout western Europe, into North America and more recently into Japan and the rest of South-East Asia. With the changing political situation in eastern Europe, Crystal Clear Ltd has set up a distribution arm to serve this emerging market. A few years ago, the company acquired a leading maker of fine china tableware. This dovetailed perfectly as both china and crystal glass tend to be sold through department stores and specialist china shops, both companies' brands are prestigious and their products premium priced, predominantly bought as giftware items.

In North America, Crystal Clear's marketing department has identified five market segments:

■ general giftware for anniversaries, retirements, birthdays, romantic inter-ludes, public holidays and festivals;
■ weddings, when young couples start collecting more expensive homeware;
■ investment giftware where items are bought both for their intrinsic beauty and for their latent accruing value – a market exploited well by Lalique;
■ business gifts and incentives for promotions; and
■ specials such as sporting trophies.

Although Crystal Clear sells into all five segments, the core markets in terms of sales volumes and profits are the general giftware segment, supported by the weddings segment. In these segments, Crystal Clear is positioned at the premium end, controlling its choice of retail outlets with care. Research in these segments reveals its brands are as sought after as Rolex watches or Chanel perfume, and as famous as Rolls Royce or Bollinger.

The marketing department, however, has additionally prioritised an emerging segment: business gifts and incentives used in sales promotions – a business-to-business market. Already worth over £30 million in the UK each year for china and glass items alone, this market is growing rapidly in North America. The task, though, is not so straightforward. Although business customers and contacts are aware of Crystal Clear's brands, they are not making consumer purchases from department stores for gifts or weddings. They are looking to give their companies' customers and suppliers gifts which reflect well on their business, are items whose value will not offend but whose recipients will not balk at the business's expense. For promotions, the choice of incentive must reflect the value of the product being promoted and its target market's values. In both areas – business giftware and incentives for promotions – competition for Crystal Clear is very different from that experienced in its traditional core markets. In these areas, the competition comes from anything as diverse as a golf weekend, theatre tickets, Air Miles to pens or clothing, not just from the rival china and crystal brands such as Royal Doulton or Waterford.

Products chosen to pitch at such customers must reflect these nuances. Pricing has to consider rival china and crystal offers as well as the myriad of competing products. Distribution is not through department stores or specialist china shops; it is through agents and predominantly direct selling. Promotion is not centred on television advertising and fashionable magazines such as *Vogue*; it is geared to direct mail shots, features in trade and the business-to-business press, and to inserts in such titles. While Crystal Clear depends on the qualities of people to sell all of its products in every segment, in this target market it has direct control having its own small direct selling team. Customer handling and service, therefore, are its own responsibility.

Having identified this as a core target market and aware of its different complexion, the task facing these marketers is the formulation of a bespoke marketing programme. Examples are given based on Crystal Clear Ltd in each chart throughout this chapter by way of an illustrative example for these charts' requirements.

P1.3.2 Products

The *product* element of the marketing mix covers several issues:

- specification of products/their attributes;
- requirements for the augmented product;
- determination of a product mix;
- branding policy;
- product positioning;
- new product development; and
- product deletion.

For most businesses, there will be an existing range of products. However, the enhanced understanding of key customer needs (KCVs), market trends and competitors' activity may have indicated the need to:

a) modify the product offered,

b) add new products to the portfolio, and

c) delete or run down some existing products.

In addition to the actual product sold, there will be a bundle of additional or ancillary features – the augmented product – which will be expected by customers or distributors, or which will help give an edge over competitors: support issues such as sales assistance, packaging, delivery, payment terms, installation, warranty and after-sales back up. These aspects are covered under P1.3.6.

The business's brand must be clearly perceived by target customers to stand for specific values: it needs a clear identity. The brand and the business's products must be positioned in the minds of targeted customers in line with their needs and expectations, the business's recommended positioning strategy (Chart S1.3) and competitors' products or services. While such brand positioning is communicated through the promotional mix, product attributes must match customers' expectations, having the appropriate specification and accompanying attributes.

Action: Products

The required *Product Mix* must be specified per target market, particularly if additional products or derivatives are required. Use Chart P1.3 to summarise the required product mix per target market, including any new products or product modifications.

P1.3.3 Price

Under the *price* element of the marketing mix there are a number of issues to consider:

- price levels;
- price 'relativities' within the overall product range;
- margin implications and cost structures;
- price positioning versus competitors and customer expectations;
- discounting and rebate policies;
- credit facilities;
- price variations subject to markets (e.g. 'home' and 'export') and customer type (e.g. key accounts);
- bid/negotiated pricing versus list prices; and
- direct sales or transfer prices for subsidiary/sister companies/ departments.

Chart P1.3 *Summary of Required Product/Service Mix per Target Market*

Segment	Existing Products/Services	Newly Required Products (With Reason Why Needed)
1 *Business Gifts–Specials*	*'Violet' collection* *'Royal' range* *'For You' parts 1 – 49*	*Range of crystal figurines to combat Doulton* *Revised range of crystal stemware to overtake Waterford*
2		
3		
4		
5		
6		
7		
8		

Actions:
- List out in column 2 the business's existing products which are 'right' for each segment targeted.
- In column 3, list out any additional/new/modified products which - in the light of the marketing analyses - are necessary to maintain the business's competitive position and to facilitate the desired target market strategy. If new products, briefly describe their core features and the reasons why they are required.

Price levels must be specified which reflect:

a) the desired positioning versus competitors,

b) targeted customer expectations,

c) price points for other products in the business's portfolio and their brand positioning, and

d) internal cost structures and required profit margins.

In addition, most businesses operate some form of large order rebate, preferential customer discounting or residual value guarantee. It is necessary to consider the business's policy on such issues. The agreed pricing levels must permit such policies. Thought should be given to the required credit policy.

There may be published list prices. In some markets these are rigid, while in others there is room for negotiation. In many business-to-business markets and services, there is the need to formally bid or negotiate pricing and contracts. It is important to determine policies which ensure these tasks are professionally undertaken in line with the determined strategy's needs. Those involved with pricing and negotiations must reflect the identified key customer values (KCVs), the business's desired brand positioning and any strengths or differential advantages (DAs).

Consider whether for 'internal' markets – transfers between departments or to sister companies – sales should be at commercial rates or at internal, preferential rates. They could be direct sales or internal transfers, but there must be a policy.

Action: Pricing

For *Pricing*, state for each product sold, in each target market, the average current achieved retail price and the desired list price, indicating the discrepancy between desired list price and achieved retail price. In order to understand the relative weaknesses of the business, repeat this exercise for the leading competitor in the target market, by product. Finally, request any overall fine-tuning or changes in the company's pricing policy (and payment terms, etc.) for the target markets under review. See Chart P1.4.

Chart P1.4 **Summary of Pricing Policy Changes**

Segment	The Business			Principal Competitor			
	Achieved Price (A)	Desired Price (D)	A-D (+/−)	Product Name	Achieved Price (A)	List Price (L)	A-L (+/−)
Business Gifts – Specials	*Violet* $35 av.	*Violet* $37 av.	− $2	*Diana, Co. X.*	$37 av.	$38 av.	− $1.
Business Gifts – Specials	*Royal* $44 av.	*Royal* $46 av.	− $2	*Niagara, Co. Y.*	$43 av.	$46 av.	− $3.
Business Gifts – Specials	*For You* $25 av.	*For You* $25	$0	*Just Now, Co. X.*	$22 av.	$25 av.	− $3

Summary of Required Pricing Changes and Pricing Policy Alterations

'For You' range is on target and improvement in margins unlikely.
Both 'Violet' and 'Royal' ranges are underachieving, but until brand and product awareness are improved price increase will be difficult. Sales force needs to be more proactive in conveying the value of these products, and needs to be encouraged to withdraw from such hefty bulk order discounts unless crucial for a particular order.
Sales team must realise different ranges attract separate pricing policies and that each segment has its own KCVs.

Actions:
- Inevitably the analyses will have revealed the need to modify pricing – for each product in each segment, so state the desired price.
- The stated strategy will also require changes to pricing/payment/credit policies; summarise these in the lower section of Chart P1.4.

P1.3.4 Place – Distribution

The *place* element of the marketing mix concerns distribution or channels to market:

- optimum channel(s) to serve each target market;

- identification of the most appropriate combination of channel members (distributors and dealers; agents and brokers; wholesalers and retailers);
- building of relationships with selected channel members;
- managing the exchange of goods, finance, information between the channel members;
- power and control over the channel to market;
- delivery times/frequencies/sizes/reliability; and
- distribution networks, stockholding and transport fleets.

Marketing channel intermediaries (members) are necessary to ensure the flows of most products or services from their point of manufacture to their consumers. It is important to have a distribution channel which reflects customer needs, the brand positioning, competitors' policies and is in line with market trends. Having determined the optimum channel it is vital to consider who are the players within it and with which ones the business should deal. There are a number of options: the business may aim to own its channel (own dealers or retail outlets); have agreements with independent channel companies (e.g. wholesalers or retailers); or be dependent on the goodwill and orders from key channel members (e.g. major dealer groups or national retail chains). It is important to understand where the balance of power lies: with the business or with another channel member. Thought should be given as to who needs to control and police the channel to ensure the business's policies are carried through and customers are satisfied with the business's products.

Delivery times, frequencies, shipment sizes and reliability may be key customer values. Even where they are not top of the list of KCVs, they are important customer satisfaction criteria. From a service perspective, along with stockholding and transport policies, they are also revisited under P1.3.6 below. The initial focus, under *place*, is the distribution network and the selection of the correct channels to be able to service the selected target market segments.

Action: Place (Distribution)

Channels to market (Distribution): on the chart provided (see Chart P1.5) summarise any changes now required to the business's distribution (e.g. more/less dealers; different distribution channel; better training; firmer, product by product objectives; incentives, etc.) and for the service elements of distribution: stockholding, delivery policies, transportation.

Chart P1.5 **Summary of Distribution Requirements**

Target Market Segment: *Business Gifts – Specials*

Marketing Channel Description
Direct selling through own sales team. Predominantly teleselling with some personal visits.

Marketing Channel Changes
None, but sales team must recognise each segment's KCVs and nature of competitive threat.

Stockholding/Inventory Requirements
Low inventory holdings have occasionally led to long lead times and a few lost orders. This needs examining.

Delivery Requirements
Current DHL contract is up for renegotiation. FedEx now pitching. For major, regular clients, must cost out establishing own transport fleet.

Transportation Issues
Currently couriers/handlers ship 100% of product in this segment. With growing sales, particularly in 3 regions, own vehicles are possible. Breakages are high, therefore shipping packaging must be up-graded.

Overall Policy Changes:
The channel is sensible, but a move to ownership of a small transport fleet in 3 regions is a major departure: costs must be assessed before next quarterly marketing executive meeting. JB to conduct formal cost-benefit analysis.

Personnel and Service Improvements Required:
- *Sales force – need orientation programme to help their understanding of segments and KCVs.*
- *Some personnel require guidelines for negotiating policy.*
- *Warehouse staff need to alter shipping packaging and respond more rapidly to replacing breakages.*

Actions:
- State the required dealer and distribution changes necessary to facilitate target market strategy and associated marketing programmes (a) per core segment, (b) overall in the territory.
- To facilitate the desired target market strategy, it is <u>essential</u> to have the understanding and co-operation of distributors/dealers; the recommendations on Chart P1.5 must reflect this.

P1.3.5 Promotion

The *promotions* element of the marketing mix concerns marketing communications:

- segment needs from promotional work;
- promotional objectives;
- target audiences;
- promotional sources and messages;
- promotional mix ingredients;
- planning the campaign;
- managing the promotional campaign;
- briefing/handling suppliers;
- determining promotional budgets; and
- evaluating the effectiveness of the campaign.

Precisely what the promotional work has to achieve must be stated: the desired brand positioning, delivery of key customer values (KCVs), emphasis of any differential advantage (DA) and strengths. The promotional objectives in each segment should be clearly understood. For example, the aim may be to create a need for an innovative product, or brand awareness, a positive attitude towards the product, purchase intention, sales leads, or to overcome competitor activity. A list of possible objectives is presented in Chart P1.7.

There will be a number of target audiences, but perhaps only a selection needs to be influenced by the promotional work: customers, distributors, shareholders, the media, suppliers, the workforce, bankers, board of directors, and so on. Each target audience is likely to respond to a different message transmitted in a certain manner. Consideration must be given to these messages and to the most appropriate media of communication. The message must reflect the desired brand positioning, key customer values (KCVs) and any differential advantage (DA).

Decisions are required concerning which ingredients of the *promotional mix* will work best to appeal to the target audience(s) and convey the determined promotional message:

- *Advertising*: using mass media such as TV, radio, cinema, press/magazines, outdoor sites or transport;
- *Personal Selling*: face-to-face contact through the sales force;
- *Sales Promotions*: such as point-of-sale displays, price cuts, free merchandise, incentives, competitions, special offers, collectibles, on-pack displays, sales literature and trade shows/exhibitions;

- *Public Relations and Publicity*;
- *Direct Mail* or *Sponsorship*.

In most instances, a selection of such tools will be appropriate and used in conjunction with each other.

Once selected, these tools have to be used in an on-going, orchestrated campaign with carefully selected media appropriate to the target audience's behaviour. To construct and manage a campaign, many businesses will contract external suppliers for all or part of the work. Large advertising agencies and public relations consultancies can undertake all of this work, from identifying target audiences, determining campaign messages, selecting ingredients of the promotional mix, choosing and booking the ideal media slots, to producing the associated stimulus material.

Promotional budgets are often the largest individual element of a marketing department's budget. They must be controlled and kept to a minimum. Following this logical process of identifying promotional objectives, understanding target audiences, determining specific campaign messages which reflect the desired brand positioning and which emphasise any differential advantage, selecting ingredients of the promotional mix and linking them in a well structured campaign, helps to effectively utilise resources. Each target segment is likely to require its own promotional campaign, although there may be some production and media economies of scale between products in several segments. Benchmarks must be set for all promotional activity – a sales target, market share gain, or brand awareness improvement – so that the spend on promotion can be evaluated and justified. This will allow for changes in activity to bring improvements in subsequent seasons.

Action: Promotion

Promotional Programmes are one of the mainstays of sales and marketing activity. First summarise what promotional work and campaigns have been running recently (do not assume everyone who should know does!). Then state the promotional objectives for any promotional work now needed (e.g. to build brand awareness; reposition a product against competitors; promote a dealer; emphasise a particular application, etc.). Finally, suggest suitable promotional programmes (e.g. trade shows, literature, advertising in specific titles, etc.) and required scheduling: everyone has expertise and knowledge to contribute here. Use Charts P1.6 to P1.8 which provide summary formats.

Chart P1.6 **Summary of Current Advertising and Promotion**

Nature of Campaign *Business Gifts – Specials*
What was done, when, which promotional mix elements
- *February, September, December inserts in 'Business Quarterly', 'Marketing Age', 'Society & Business'.*
- *Mail shot in October to 10,000 businesses on GL News's list.*
- *On-going teleselling, with drives based on GL News's list in February and November.*
- *Classified adverts each issue in 'Business Quarterly', 'Marketing Age', 'Society & Business', 'Business Today', 'Stockmarket Monthly'.*

Campaign Objectives
For example, create brand awareness; generate sales leads; counteract rival's campaign; support new product launch; assist dealer promotion; etc.
- *Create sales leads*
- *Create brand or product awareness*
- *Help establish market potential*

Cost of Programme (if known)
- *Inserts*   *Printing $15,000; Distribution $105,000*
- *Mail shot*   *Distribution $30,000; Printing $15,000*
- *Teleselling*   *Not known*
- *Classified ads*   *$8,500 quarterly*

Results of Programme (if known)
Sales by volume up 12%
Repeat business from businesses on GL News's list up 40%
Impact of separate promotional activities not known yet!

Action:
- Complete a form per targeted segment summarising the existing promotional work being undertaken.

Chart P1.7 **Key Promotional Activity Required**

Promotional Task	Targeted Segments							
	1 *Business Gifts – Specials*	**2**	**3**	**4**	**5**	**6**	**7**	**8**
Build brand awareness	✓✓✓							
Build brand image	✓							
Build product awareness	✓✓							
Build product image	✓							
Position against competitors	✓							
Reposition against competitors								
Create primary demand for product								
Influence customers' KCVs								
Generate sales leads	✓							
Promote after sales support								
Promote dealers/ distributors								
Support dealers' promotions								
Promote customer credit								
Influence customer buying process								
Other: *Tie in with sales team drives*	✓							
Other:								

Actions:

- Indicate promotional requirements per targeted segment.
- Keep selections to the bare minimum - too many will not be feasible or cost effective.
- If most rows in a column are ticked, revisit the list to prioritise and to reduce the selection.

Chart P1.8 **Desired Promotional Programmes**

Target Segment: *Business Gifts – Specials*

Promotion Objectives (priorities)
Brand awareness in this segment
Product awareness/understanding
Sales leads

Suggested Advertising and Promotions Programmes
(Actual promotional tools)
- *Examine customer records; re-assess choice of media titles, continue inserts accordingly. Continuously assess levels of response per title.*
- *Similarly reconsider choice of titles for classified, then continue weekly or monthly.*
- *Attend 'Incentives Today' trade show.*
- *Target newly selected key media titles for PR coverage – PR Ace Inc to assist.*
- *Structure sales drives to fit into seasonality of this business and to phase with PR/advertising exposure.*

Anticipated Budget Required
As current year, plus $15,000 for 'Incentives Today', $7,000 for tracking research, $30,000 for PR Ace Inc's retainer.

Timing and Scheduling of Promotional Activity
Press inserts to phase before each sales peak (e.g.: Sept/Oct for Christmas). Classified continuously. PR to support inserts but also to help level out seasonal lows. Tracking research now as a priority. PR briefings now.

Actions:
- Complete a form per targeted segment.
- Ensure the recommendations reflect KCVs, desired brand positioning and the competitive position.

P1.3.6 People – Service

The *people* element of the marketing mix invariably is linked to aspects of *customer service*:

- required service levels;
- implications for personnel;
- staffing levels and abilities;
- staff selection, training and motivation;
- orientation of personnel specifically to this segmentation study's strategic and operational recommendations; and
- augmented product considerations.

It will be necessary to determine the required *Service Levels* to support the product mix: see Charts P1.9 and P1.10. There may be recruitment and training implications for the business's personnel (Chart P1.9).

Personnel need carefully selecting, training and motivating. In the context of this segmentation work, they need orienting towards the aims of the target market strategy and the key messages which must be communicated to targeted segments and to marketing channel members. Inevitably, there will be some training requirements associated with any new segmentation scheme.

Aspects of the augmented product (see P1.3.2) determine customers' perception of customer satisfaction and are important concerns when considering *people*: the business's personnel are responsible for sales assistance, packaging, stockholding, delivery (times, frequencies, sizes, reliability, transport policies), installation, warranty and after-sales support, plus payment and credit arrangements. Many of these issues have been covered in Charts P1.3 and P1.5.

Action: People – Service

Determine the required *service levels* and *people* issues to support the rest of the marketing mix using Charts P1.9 and P1.10. Aspects of the augmented product have by now been addressed in Charts P1.3 and P1.5.

Chart P1.9 Required Service Levels to Support Product Mix

	Segment 1: Business Gifts – Specials	Segment 2:	Segment 3:	Segment 4:
People	1 more salesperson. New supervisor. Upgraded workforce supervision			
Advice/ Guidance (not consultancy)				
On-Going Support	Teleselling to maintain links with clients, hence 1 new person			
Facilities	New IT system for mailing lists/ teleselling			
Other:				
Other:				

Any Training Requirements?
- *Orientation for salesforce/handling of existing clients*
- *Instructions for warehouse staff*
- *Training for salesforce on new IT system*

Resource/Recruitment Implications
1 new person in sales – now
PR Ace Inc to help with orientation, supporting Marketing Director
IT supplier to provide on-site training, therefore no recruitment, and no additional cost. Note: training will interfere with selling time for sales operators.

Actions:
- This table requests information concerning service aspects of the product offer. The products *per se* (their tangible attributes) are detailed in Chart P1.3.
- Some service aspects will require retraining/orientation of personnel interfacing with customers, so state these requirements.
- These 'soft' issues connected with the product offering inevitably will require resourcing.

Chart P1.10 **Process/Customer Liaison Improvements Required**

Area Requiring Attention	Explanation/ Definition	Required Action
Market Information	*Competitive position* } *to* *Price comparisons* } *customers*	*JB to instigate* *JB to conduct*
Product Information		
Flows of information for Bids/Pricing		
Demonstrations	*Don't do any. Must attend trade shows*	*JB to set up*
Handling Enquiries	*OK, but new systems should help*	*KD to monitor*
Pre-Delivery Advice (e.g. Progress Meetings)		
Commercial Support to Customers		
Technical Support		
Back-up Advice		
Payment Conditions		
Inter-personnel Relationships	*Sales force must get better at this*	*KD to set up training in New Year*
Communication With Clients	*Not good with existing clients*	*JB is on to this one!*
Handling Visits		
Communication With Suppliers		
Feedback to Clients/Suppliers		
Other:		
Other:		

Actions:
- This is the business helping customers; making life easier for customers to deal with the business; improving flows of information and communications - specify such required improvements.

P1.4 Summary

The marketing mix forms the core of a marketing programme. By addressing each of the elements of the marketing mix per segment, the basis of the implementation programmes has been created: products, pricing, place/distribution, promotion, people/service. These actions and recommendations must reflect the identified KCVs and competitive position, and be geared to facilitate the desired brand positioning in each segment.

P1 Checklist: Marketing Programmes

Please read and complete the following checklist.

1. What you should have determined:

Before moving on to the next chapter you should have developed a separate marketing mix for each targeted segment. This marketing mix should include details of the product mix required, pricing policies and levels, distribution needs, promotional plans, people and customer service needs. In other words, the detailed actions required for the business to properly address each target market. The recommended marketing mix ingredients must aim to satisfy customers' needs (KCVs), emphasise any differential advantage (DA) or strengths held by the business, achieve its desired brand positioning versus rivals and implement the recommended target market strategy (see S1.4).

You cannot complete the segmentation process or implement the recommended target market strategy without thoroughly working through the required marketing mix for each segment targeted.

2. Charts which should have been completed:

Make a record of your progress in completing the following charts:

	Status of Analysis		
	Complete	Partly filled	Not complete
P1.1: Summary by Segment of KCVs and DAs	❏	❏	❏
P1.2: Customer Perceptions Versus Leading Rivals	❏	❏	❏
P1.3: Summary of Required Product/Service Mix	❏	❏	❏
P1.4: Summary of Pricing Policy Changes	❏	❏	❏
P1.5: Summary of Distribution/Channel Requirements	❏	❏	❏
P1.6: Summary of Current Advertising and Promotion	❏	❏	❏
P1.7: Key Promotional Activity Required	❏	❏	❏
P1.8: Desired Promotional Programmes	❏	❏	❏
P1.9: Required Service Levels to Support Product Mix	❏	❏	❏
P1.10: Process/Customer Liaison Improvements Required	❏	❏	❏

These charts must now be completed.

3. Information required:

The following areas of information are required for work in this chapter. See Chart S1.4.

	Information
	Collected
Target market priority list	❏
Target market strategy summary	❏
KCVs to satisfy per segment	❏
Strengths/weaknesses per segment	❏
Any DAs to emphasise in marketing programmes	❏
Desired brand positioning to achieve	❏

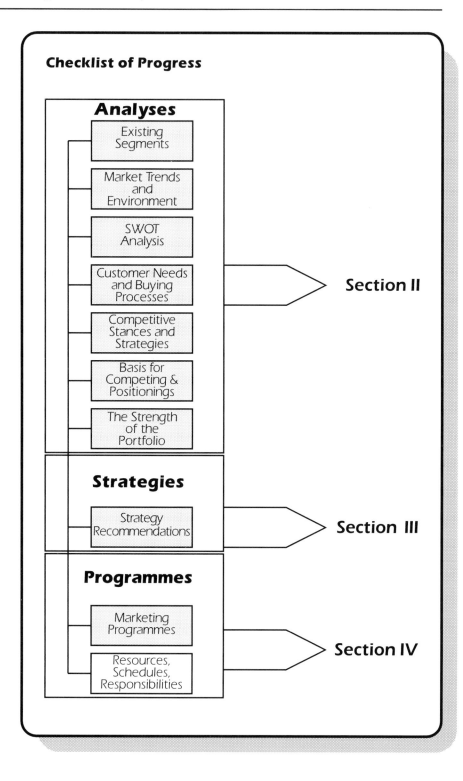

Checklist of Progress

Analyses

- Existing Segments
- Market Trends and Environment
- SWOT Analysis
- Customer Needs and Buying Processes
- Competitive Stances and Strategies
- Basis for Competing & Positionings
- The Strength of the Portfolio

Section II

Strategies

- Strategy Recommendations

Section III

Programmes

- Marketing Programmes
- Resources, Schedules, Responsibilities

Section IV

P2

Resources, Schedules, Responsibilities, Implications and On-Going Requirements

P2.1 Introduction

Chapter P1 has presented detailed action plans. Unless personnel are allocated to manage each task with clear time frames and the necessary budgets, implementation of the marketing programmes cannot be guaranteed. Attention now needs to be given to the control of these programmes.

Some of the recommendations will result in the business making few changes to the current marketing activity, while some programme requirements will be quite a departure from existing practices. The overall direction must be orchestrated within clear guidelines, time-frames and budgets. The detail must be allocated to individual managers to ensure that tasks are carried out.

The marketing function will have been responsible for determining the target market strategy and its required marketing programmes. Inevitably these market segment strategy recommendations for target marketing and supportive marketing programmes will have some impact on other functions within the business, such as R&D, Production, Shipping, Finance, Personnel. It is important to understand these knock-on effects and their importance. For example, will other departments need to alter/update their practices? Do they need to be aware of certain market developments determined during the analyses? It is vital that other functional areas in the business are committed to the process and aware of the segmentation issues if implementation is to be successfully achieved.

No matter how efficient and well resourced the business, not all issues raised during the segmentation process can be addressed immediately. Certain aspects take time, such as new product development, policy changes and some marketing intelligence gathering.

Chapter P2 also discusses an important additional aspect of the control process – the monitoring of progress and assessing effectiveness. The chapter concludes with a warning: there will be inevitable internal barriers to implementation success. Consideration, in advance, of these issues will help to overcome any hurdles.

The simple charts presented in this chapter act as a control mechanism, ensuring the programmes do not, however fleetingly, disappear from view and that management acts to implement them.

By the end of this chapter you will have considered resourcing the recommended marketing programmes, scheduling the activities and allocating responsibilities to individual managers or departments. In addition, you will have explored any knock-on ramifications from the recommendations on other parts of the business together with on-going work requirements such as product development, training and marketing research. Thought will have been given to establishing benchmarks against which progress can be measured. Any likely internal barriers facing successful implementation of the plans will have been highlighted.

P2.2 Resources, Schedules and Responsibilities

To be actioned, the marketing programmes detailed in chapter P1 will require budgets. The programmes must be put together in carefully scheduled timetables and personnel or departments need to be allocated to each task to ensure the activities take place.

Summarise in Chart P2.1 the marketing programme tasks detailed in Charts P1.3 to P1.10 of the previous chapter, the personnel to be responsible for actioning them, timing (scheduling) and anticipated cost.

Chart P2.1 **Summary of Programme Tasks, Timing and Costs**

Programme Task	Person or Department Responsible	Date(s) for Activity	Anticipated Cost	Implications to the Business

Actions:
- The main marketing mix requirements from chapter P1 must be entered in column 1.
- People must now take 'ownership' of identified actions from chapter P1.

It may be necessary to consolidate these implementation details into summary statements of responsibilities by name/department, by month, and under convenient budget headings: see Charts P2.2 and P2.3, for example.

Chart P2.2 *Summary of Responsibilities*

Person or Department	Responsibility/Task	Dates/Timings

Actions:
- Allocate the tasks detailed in Chart P2.1 to individual managers or departments.
- Specify when these activities must take place.

Summarise the total budgetary requirements from the marketing programmes detailed in chapter P1. Do these combined costs have any wider implications for the business?

Chart P2.3 *Summary of Costs and Budget Implications*

Task	Cost	Any Budget Implications for the Business?

Actions:
- Summarise the costs/budgets for each of the marketing programme activities detailed in chapter P1.
- Outline any implications from the combined totals of these costs.

P2.3 Associated Implications

Inevitably there will be some resulting ramifications from the recommended target market strategy and proposed marketing programmes. A number of areas of the business may be affected, including R&D, Production, Shipping, Finance, Personnel. The nature and scope of these knock-on effects must be addressed and attention focused on those departments which will need to alter/update their practices. It may be necessary to make these departments aware of relevant market developments determined during the analyses.

To be implemented successfully, all other functional areas in the business need to be consulted and aware of the segmentation issues stemming from this process.

To ensure that this happens, raise any associated implications of the strategy recommendations and marketing programmes for:

a) the business as a whole,

b) individual departments,

c) any sister companies/product groups,

briefly in Chart P2.4.

Make sure that named individuals are charged with addressing these issues.

Chart P2.4 *Summary of Likely Areas of Impacts*

Area of Impact	Implication/Required Action? By whom?

Action:
• Detail the likely knock-on impacts.

P2.4 On-Going Needs

No matter how efficient and well-resourced the business, not all issues raised during the segmentation process can be addressed immediately. Certain aspects take time, such as new product development, policy changes and marketing intelligence gathering.

P2.4.1 Marketing Research Requirements

The analyses will have identified weaknesses or gaps in the business's information (see Chart P2.5), perhaps in terms of customers' needs or buying practices, competitors' strategies, brand perceptions or market trends. These issues can be tackled by deciding the nature of information required, timing and probable method of data collection.

Chart P2.5   On-Going Marketing Research Requirements

Information Gap	Likely Research Activity	Timing	Cost

Action:
- Specify required marketing research activity.

P2.4.2 Longer-Term Marketing Mix Requirements

There will be many issues raised by the analyses, strategy recommendations and marketing programmes which cannot be addressed immediately, such as internal structuring or operations, product ranges and customer service, marketing programmes and market development. These issues must be clearly stated, otherwise these deficiencies will not be dealt with. Use Chart P2.6 to summarise this on-going work.

Chart P2.6 On-Going Work Required Summary

Area	Required Work
Internal Structuring/ Operations	
Market Development	
Resource Base	
Products and Product Mix	
Sales Force and Customer Service	
People Issues	
Distribution and Dealers	
Promotional Activity/ Evaluation	
Pricing and Payment Terms	

P2.5 Monitoring the Effectiveness of the Target Market Plan

The final stage of the segmentation exercise is to ensure that procedures are set up for monitoring the effectiveness of the plan. There are two parts to this important stage of the process.

First, a periodic review must be conducted to determine whether the stated target market objectives (Chart S1.4) have been achieved. Make a note of when the reviews will take place, what form they should follow and who will be involved. Formalising this part of the monitoring will help ensure that the review really happens. It is also important to check that the strategy is improving the financial health and status of the business.

The second part of the monitoring process involves systematically updating the marketing analyses (Section II) as more information becomes available. Customer needs, competitors' strategies, market trends, SWOTs, bases for competing and brand positionings will all be subject to change over time. By incorporating new information into the analyses, a useful impression is gained of the more subtle changes brought about by implementing the target market strategy.

It may be useful to complete Chart P2.7 to identify the business's performance in relation to the strategy objectives set and other areas considered to be important. The monitored issues column has been left blank enabling a choice of areas to revisit.

Chart P2.7 **Monitoring Performance**

Monitored Issue	Expected Result (6 mths)	Actual Outcome (6 mths)	Reason for Gap	Expected Result (12 mths)	Actual Outcome (12 mths)	Reason for Gap

Actions:
- Determine measures for benchmarking progress.
- Expected results should include sales, contributions, attitudinal data relating to customers' perceptions of brand positioning (versus stated desired positioning in Chart S1.3) and their views on customer satisfaction.

P2.6 Anticipating Implementation Problems

Determining the desired marketing programmes to facilitate the implementation of the recommended target market strategy is no guarantee of successful execution. Research shows that there are often internal barriers to overcome if the business's senior management and non-marketing business functions are to respond to the strategies and tactics.

Very often those involved in planning and in producing the target market recommendations are divorced from central management and chief executive. Marketing personnel may be too optimistic or carried along by the fervour of the marketing analyses. Too much attention may be devoted to the analyses with implementation issues being rushed through at the last moment. Even the marketing programmes may be put together in haste. Marketers may deliberately ignore likely implementation hurdles, choosing instead to focus on the analyses and interesting recommendations. Worse, implementation may be acknowledged as difficult and – despite thoughtful analyses and sensible strategies – abandoned.

Warning signs which may signal potential difficulties with implementation include:

- marketers too distant/divorced from senior management;
- unrealistic optimism by marketers;
- skating over the analyses;
- too much attention to the analyses and strategies;
- insufficient time devoted to revising the required marketing programmes;
- denial of implementation problems; and
- avoidance of difficult issues/changes.

In order to ensure that implementation occurs smoothly, personnel involved in the segmentation work must:

1. Think through barriers to successful implementation.

2. Offer clear time frames to colleagues for implementation.

3. Be clear about expected results/benchmarks.

4. Be realistic in recommendations and expectations.

5. Address priority problems.

6. 'Grease' the package of recommendations/actions by *positioning* the central themes.

7. Identify key players outside the marketing function.

8. Regularly orientate other functional areas and senior management, involving key players in the analyses and target prioritisation.

9. Monitor the views of the key players.

10. Communicate at all times with senior management and colleagues.

The 'problems to overcome' listed in charts S1.4 and S1.5 are a useful starting point, as these will include some internal/political barriers to implementation. There must be a discussion to highlight any likely resistance to change and any hurdles blocking the effective and smooth implementation of the target market strategy and its associated marketing programmes. Realism is the key. Significant shifts in the business's emphasis may not be accepted immediately. In addition, with altered customer groups and revised target priorities, there inevitably will be some personnel averse to change.

Regular orientation of key decision-makers in the business and effective communication within the business are essential ingredients for successful implementation of the action programmes. As with any product or service, the results of the market segmentation work must be *positioned in the minds* of target personnel *within* the business (as well as to customers, distributors, the media, shareholders and other external target audiences) and communicated.

P2.7 Summary

In this chapter you will have concluded the implementation programmes and therefore completed the analysis, strategy, programmes for implementation – ASP – segmentation process. Specifically, you will have allocated budgets, time frames and personnel to each of the marketing mix activities; considered any implications from these activities for other parts of the business; determined on-going work requirements; established benchmarks against which to monitor the progress of the target market strategy, and considered potential internal hurdles to overcome to facilitate implementation of the recommended plans. Good luck!

P2 Checklist: Resources, Schedules, Responsibilities, Implications and On-Going Requirements

Please read and complete the following checklist.

1. What you should have undertaken:

Before the marketing mix recommendations can be implemented, the marketing actions need formalising into programmes of activity. In this chapter you should have determined marketing budgets, allocated resources, determined time-frames for the activities and allocated responsibility for actioning the specific recommendations to individual managers or departments.

There will be ramifications from these marketing programmes for other areas of the business. There will be certain issues which cannot be tackled immediately but on which work must continue, such as product development, training and recruitment or marketing research. Some attempt must be made to assess the progress of implementing the desired target market strategy and for judging its effectiveness. Finally, there will be internal barriers to successful implementation which must be considered. These issues are all integral to the implementation of the determined marketing mixes and are addressed in this chapter. The segmentation work is not complete until these issues have been tackled.

2. Charts which should have been completed:

Make a record of your progress in completing the following charts:

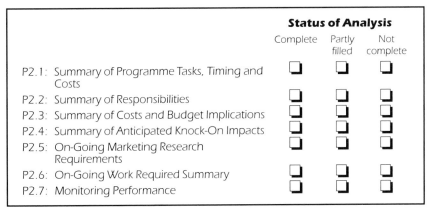

	Status of Analysis		
	Complete	Partly filled	Not complete
P2.1: Summary of Programme Tasks, Timing and Costs	❏	❏	❏
P2.2: Summary of Responsibilities	❏	❏	❏
P2.3: Summary of Costs and Budget Implications	❏	❏	❏
P2.4: Summary of Anticipated Knock-On Impacts	❏	❏	❏
P2.5: On-Going Marketing Research Requirements	❏	❏	❏
P2.6: On-Going Work Required Summary	❏	❏	❏
P2.7: Monitoring Performance	❏	❏	❏

These must now be completed in full.

3. Information required:

Marketing Mix Tasks from chapter P1

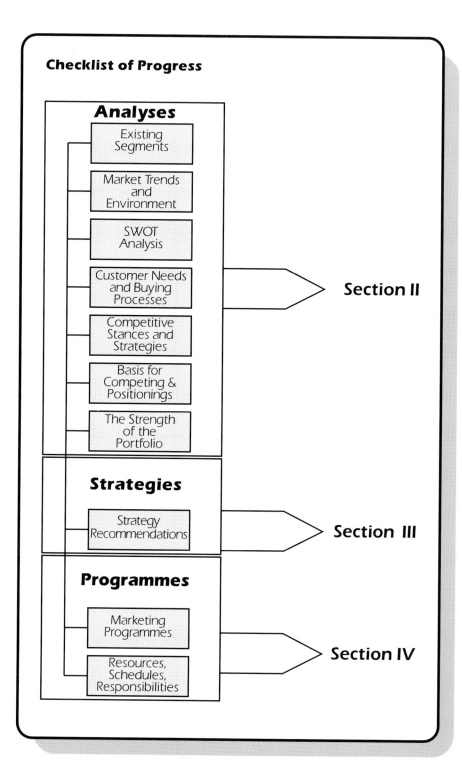

Checklist of Progress

Analyses

- Existing Segments
- Market Trends and Environment
- SWOT Analysis
- Customer Needs and Buying Processes
- Competitive Stances and Strategies
- Basis for Competing & Positionings
- The Strength of the Portfolio

Section II

Strategies

- Strategy Recommendations

Section III

Programmes

- Marketing Programmes
- Resources, Schedules, Responsibilities

Section IV

End Piece

This text has been designed as a workbook to take managers through the essential steps required when re-evaluating target markets. The starting premise is that few managers will have a blank sheet of paper: most businesses will have existing customer groupings defined with which sales, marketing and distribution are already operating. Changes to these groupings need to be sensible, constructive and acceptable to managers. Following through the chapters of this book should lead to changes which move the business on, capitalise on any competitive edge and are based on reasoned argument palatable to the most risk-averse sales manager.

The essential stages have been broken down into three sets of activities: Analyses in Section II, Strategy Decisions in Section III, and Programmes for Implementation in Section IV. Background explanation is presented in Section I.

By the end of this book you should have:

- reviewed the business's existing customer base and groupings;
- considered market trends and the marketing environment;
- assessed the business's strengths, weaknesses, opportunities and threats;
- understood customers' needs, buying processes and influences;
- evaluated competitors' strategies, differential advantages and competitive positions;
- considered the business's basis for competing and its perceived brand positioning; and
- examined the business's product portfolio.

These are essential marketing analyses to undertake for any formal marketing initiative. They are fundamental to reassessing target markets. Full guidance is given for attempting each analysis.

Once these analyses are complete, the information must be used to make important strategic decisions:

- revision of customer groupings;
- determination of market segments;
- selection of priority target markets;
- defensible differential advantages;
- desired brand positionings; and

- problems to overcome.

With the target market strategy then in place, marketing programmes must be developed which implement the recommended strategy:

- product requirements,
- pricing levels and policies,
- distribution channels,
- promotional campaigns,
- people and customer service,
- budgets,
- allocation of responsibilities,
- scheduling of activities,
- on-going developments,
- monitoring progress and effectiveness, and
- handling of barriers to implementation.

Tackled comprehensively, objectively and sequentially these ASP stages should result in a number of core benefits for the business in question:

- a better understanding of customer segments and target market priorities;
- a fresh look at core markets;
- increased customer and distributor satisfaction;
- a more market-focused business;
- maximised use of company strengths;
- full utilisation of competitive edges;
- clear and appropriate use of resources;
- a sense of direction and understanding within the business; and
- enhanced internal communication across and within functions.

Once determined, this segmentation scheme should remain relevant for several years, unless something dramatic happens in the marketplace such as the entrance of a new, dominant competitor or a major economic slump. The annual marketing planning cycle adopted by most businesses should enable minor revisions to the target markets to be addressed annually by each plan's marketing programmes.

We hope you have found this book to be of assistance and wish you good luck with your market segmentation and determination of target markets.

Sally Dibb and Lyndon Simkin

Appendix

Charts for Completion

Chart A1.1 **Summary of Existing Market Segments/Sectors**

Customer Group or Segment	These Customers' Key Needs (KCVs)	Adopted Descriptions Used by Company to Describe Segment
1		
2		
3		
4		
5		
6		
7		
8		

Actions:
- Rank segments in column 1 in order of current importance to company.
- For each segment, rank the Key Customer Values listed in column 2.
- Define KCV term if required so as to avoid ambiguity.

Chart A1.2 **Historic Importance of Segments**

Rank Order of Segments by Year										
Segment	t-9	t-8	t-7	t-6	t-5	t-4	t-3	t-2	t-1	Current year (t)
1										
2										
3										
4										
5										
6										
7										
8										

Reasons for Major Changes

Actions:
- Rank each segment's importance to the business over the years. The business may view sales volumes, market share, profitability or contribution as a measure of importance.
- Explain any big moves/rank changes.

Chart A1.3 **ABC Sales: Contribution Chart**

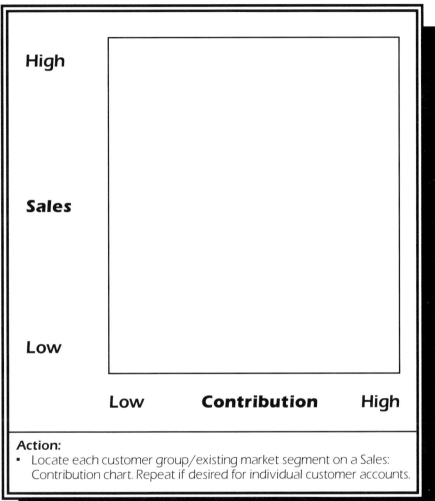

High

Sales

Low

Low   **Contribution**   High

Action:
- Locate each customer group/existing market segment on a Sales:
  Contribution chart. Repeat if desired for individual customer accounts.

Chart A2.1 **Core Market Trends and Predictions**

Year	Market Name	Sales Volumes (Units)	Sales (£s/$s)	Profit-ability (£s/$s)	Market Size	The Business's Market Share	Number of Principal Customer	Number of Principal Dealers/ Distributors
t-5								
t-4								
t-3								
t-2								
t-1								
Current year (t)								
t+1								
t+2								
t+3								
t+4								

Actions:
- Complete as many columns as possible. Sales and market share are essential.
- Information beyond the current year should be based on forecasts/estimates.
- Principal customers: most businesses have an '80:20' split – the bulk of business (e.g. '80%') comes from a minority of customers (e.g. '20%') – see ABC analysis in Chart A1.3.

Chart A2.2 **The Marketing Environment Issues**

Summary of Core Issues

Macro Environment
(legal, regulatory and political, societal, technological, economic)

Micro Environment
(direct and substitute competition, new entrants, supplier influence, customer buying power)

Principal Implications for the Business of These Issues

Actions:
- Consider the wide range of potentially relevant concerns.
- Be prudent and objective - list only important concerns.
- List the most important issues first.
- Have evidence to support these assertions.

Chart A3.1 **The SWOT Analysis**

Strengths	Weaknesses

Opportunities	Threats

Actions:
- Rank (list) points in order of importance.
- Only include key points/issues.
- Have evidence to support these points.
- Strengths and Weaknesses should be relative to main competitors.
- Strengths and Weaknesses are *internal* issues.
- Opportunities and Threats are *external*, marketing environment issues.

What are the core implications from these issues?

Chart A4.1 **Customers, KCVs, Buying Process Steps and Core Influences**

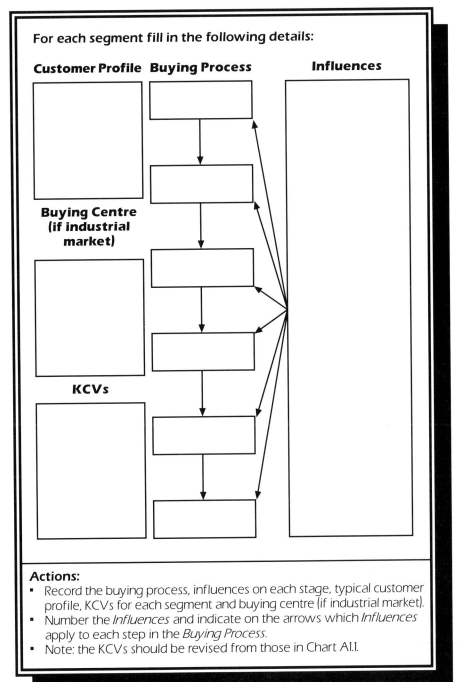

For each segment fill in the following details:

Customer Profile   Buying Process   Influences

Buying Centre (if industrial market)

KCVs

Actions:
- Record the buying process, influences on each stage, typical customer profile, KCVs for each segment and buying centre (if industrial market).
- Number the *Influences* and indicate on the arrows which *Influences* apply to each step in the *Buying Process*.
- Note: the KCVs should be revised from those in Chart A1.1.

Chart A4.2 Implications from Examining the Buying Process and KCVs

---

At which stages in the buying process are competitors active?

Are competitors maximising opportunities currently missed by the business? If so, which ones?

Implications? Are there any additional stages in the buying process the business should try to affect?

Which influencing factors can the business in turn influence?

Are there any edges over competitors in the stages already tackled by the business or influences addressed?

Actions:
- The principal benefit of the analysis in Chart A4.1 is to provoke the information used later on in the Strategy Section of this workbook to redefine segments, so the ramifications of the analysis in Chart A4.1 must be considered.
- There are, though, additional benefits in terms of learning from competitors' activities within the buying process and in addressing the influencing factors; there are edges the business will have over these rivals, plus there will be stages and people currently not targeted by the business who must be.

Chart A5.1 **Competitive Positions and Differential Advantage Overview**

Competitive Position	Segment:	Segment:	Segment:
Market Leader: • Market Share Change • KCVs Offered • DA (if any)	- - - - -	- - - - -	- - - - -
Challenger 1: • Market Share Change • KCVs Offered • DA (if any)	- - - - -	- - - - -	- - - - -
Challenger 2: • Market Share Change • KCVs Offered • DA (if any)	- - - - -	- - - - -	- - - - -
Challenger 3: • Market Share Change • KCVs Offered • DA (if any)	- - - - -	- - - - -	- - - - -
Fast Mover: • Market Share Change • KCVs Offered • DA (if any)	- - - - -	- - - - -	- - - - -
Follower: • Market Share Change • KCVs Offered • DA (if any)	- - - - -	- - - - -	- - - - -
Nicher: • Market Share change • KCVs Offered • DA (if any)	- - - - -	- - - - -	- - - - -

Actions:
- Record the competitive positions for each segment.
- The KCVs on this chart are those KCVs that each competitor is able to match.
- Most companies do not have a DA (differential advantage), so this slot may be left blank for many companies.
- There is *no* need to list actual %s for market share changes, current year versus last year. Key to market share entries: ++ large market share increase; + small market share increase; − small market share decline; −− large market share decline.

Chart A6.1 **Identification of DAs**

Segment Name	Identified Advantages (Strengths) for the Business Over Rivals	Are Advantages Sufficient Basis for a DA (Differential Advantage)?
1		
2		
3		
4		
5		
6		
7		
8		

Actions:
- Record any DAs held by the business.
- Remember a strength is only a possible DA if target customers desire it and rivals do not offer it.
- Remember that to be sufficient for a DA, the strength must be cost-effective and in the short term, defensible.

Chart A6.2 **The Positioning Map**

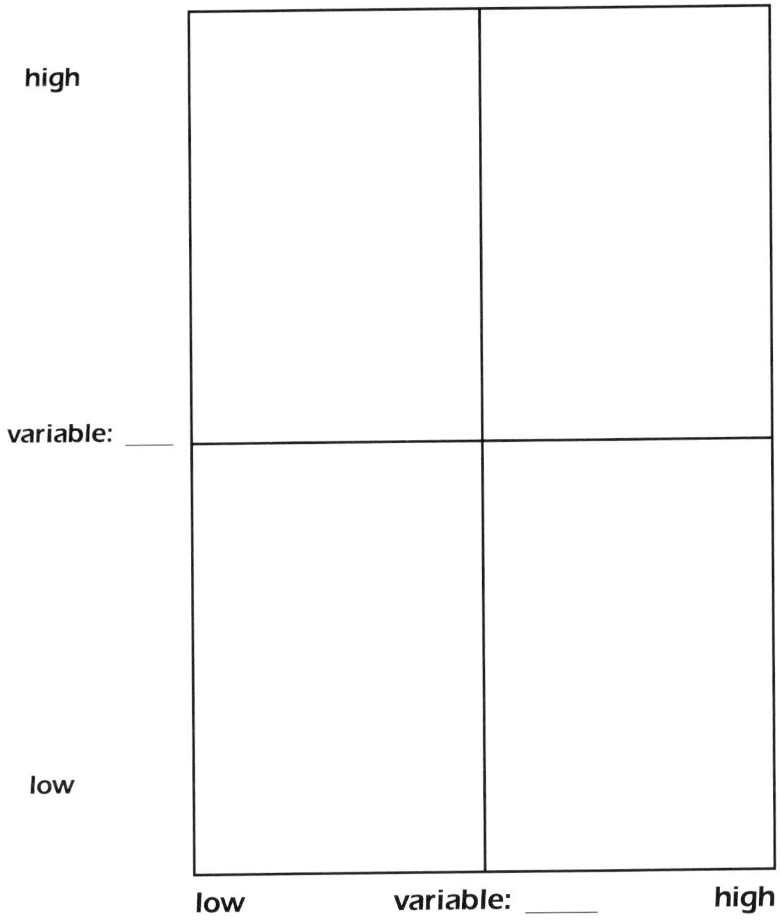

high

variable: _____

low

low   variable: _____   high

Actions:

- Let customer feedback specify the KCVs to use on the map's axes.
- Plot customers' perceptions of the relative positionings (locations) on the map of the business's brands and leading competitors' brands or products.
- Consider likely directions each player plotted may move in the near future.
- The business's desired brand positioning will be examined in Section III of the workbook.

Chart A7.1 Information Required for the DPM Analysis

Market Attractiveness

Factors	Score	Weighting	Ranking

Business/Competitive Position

Factors	Score	Weighting	Ranking

Actions:
- Select the most important factors. Complete the columns.
- This information now needs to be plotted on Chart A7.2, as in Figure A7.1.

Chart A7.2 **The DPM**

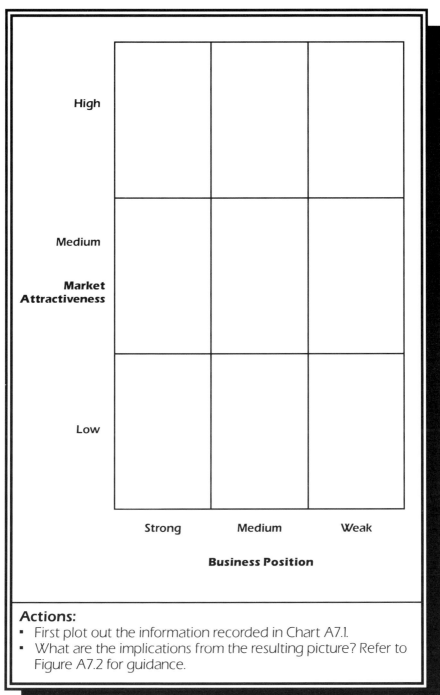

Actions:
- First plot out the information recorded in Chart A7.1.
- What are the implications from the resulting picture? Refer to Figure A7.2 for guidance.

Chart S1.1 *Summary of Segment Changes*

List of Original Customer Groups From Chart A1.1	Newly Identified Customer Groups/Segments	Explanation: Why are These New Groups/Segments so Defined?
▪	1.	?1.
▪	2.	?2.
▪	3.	?3.
▪	4.	?4.
▪	5.	?5.
▪	6.	?6.
▪	7.	?7.
▪	8.	?8.
▪	9.	?9.
▪	10.	?10.

Actions:
- Use Chart S1.1 to summarise changes to how customer groups (segments) are now defined.
- Explain in column 3 why the new segments are so defined.

Chart S1.2 **Target Segment Selection Summary**

Segment 1: _____
Segment Profile Description: _____
Why is this segment important? _____
_____
_____

Segment 2: _____
Segment Profile Description: _____
Why is this segment important? _____
_____
_____

Segment 3: _____
Segment Profile Description: _____
Why is this segment important? _____
_____
_____

Segment 4: _____
Segment Profile Description: _____
Why is this segment important? _____
_____
_____

Segment 5: _____
Segment Profile Description: _____
Why is this segment important? _____
_____
_____

Segment 6: _____
Segment Profile Description: _____
Why is this segment important? _____
_____
_____

Segment 7: _____
Segment Profile Description: _____
Why is this segment important? _____
_____
_____

Segment 8: _____
Segment Profile Description: _____
Why is this segment important? _____
_____
_____

Action:
▪ List newly determined segments in rank order of importance.

Chart S1.3 **Desired Brand Positioning**

Segment: _____

High

Variable:
_____

Low

Low   **Variable:** _____   **High**

Statement of Desired Positioning:

Actions:
- Copy existing brand positionings from Chart A6.2.
- Add the desired positioning for the business's brands in this segment. Be realistic!
- Repeat for each target segment.

Chart S1.4 **Target Market Strategy Summary Statement**

Core Target Segments						
Segment	1:	2:	3:	4:	5:	6:
Principal Reason for Segment Being Target Priority	▪	▪	▪	▪	▪	▪
Likely Sales Current Year	-	-	-	-	-	-
Likely Sales Next Year	-	-	-	-	-	-
Likely Sales in Two Years	-	-	-	-	-	-
KCVs per Segment	1 2 3 4	1 2 3 4	1 2 3 4	1 2 3 4	1 2 3 4	1 2 3 4
Major Market Opportunity	▪	▪	▪	▪	▪	▪
Principal Marketing Objective	▪	▪	▪	▪	▪	▪
Required Brand Positioning	▪	▪	▪	▪	▪	▪
Main Two Competitors	1 2	1 2	1 2	1 2	1 2	1 2
Main Competitive Threat	▪	▪	▪	▪	▪	▪
Differential Advantage (DA) Held (if any)	-	-	-	-	-	-
Key Problems to Overcome	- -	- -	- -	- -	- -	- -
Capital Implications from Strategy	▪	▪	▪	▪	▪	▪

▪ It is important to complete Chart S1.4 comprehensively: it is the overall statement of target market strategy and drives the marketing programmes.

Chart S1.5 **Tackling the Core Problems**

E.g.: Innovative packaging material

The Core Problems to Overcome					
Problem to Overcome	Segment/ Segments	Action Required	Who to Assess Problem	When to Assess	Cost Implication

Actions:

- Summarise the problems to overcome identified in Chart S1.4.
- Use Chart S1.5 to ensure these problems are tackled.

Chart P1.1 **Summary by Segment of KCVs and DAs**
E.g.: Crystal glassware/ceramics

	Segment 1:	Segment 2:	Segment 3:	Segment 4:	Segment 5:	Segment 6:
Summary of KCVs						
Main Competi- tive Threat to the Business						
Any DA Held by the Business? What?						
Desired positioning						

Chart P1.2 **Customer Perceptions Versus Leading Rivals**

	Current Perceptions for Segment:				
	Positive		Neutral	Negative	
	++	+	+/−	−	− −
Brand					
Product Image					
Product Quality					
After Sales Support					
Value of Deliverable					
Product Performance					
Product Safety					
Dealer Coverage					
Other:					
Other:					

Actions:
- Produce one form per targeted segment.
- First enter the business's rating: ++, +, +/−, − or −−. NB: ++ = very positive/ good; +/− = neutral; − − = highly negative/very poor.
- Second enter the ratings for the two leading rivals in the segment.
- Use a coding to mark companies on the chart: B = *The Business*; 1 = main rival; 2 = second main rival. Competitor 1 is: _____
  Competitor 2 is: _____

Chart P1.3 **Summary of Required Product/Service Mix per Target Market**

Segment	Existing Products/Services	Newly Required Products (With Reason Why Needed)
1		
2		
3		
4		
5		
6		
7		
8		

Actions:
- List out in column 2 the business's existing products which are 'right' for each segment targeted.
- In column 3, list out any additional/new/modified products which - in the light of the marketing analyses - are necessary to maintain the business's competitive position and to facilitate the desired target market strategy. If new products, briefly describe their core features and the reasons why they are required.

Chart P1.4 **Summary of Pricing Policy Changes**

Segment	The Business			Principal Competitor			
	Achieved Price (A)	Desired Price (D)	A-D (+/−)	Product Name	Achieved Price (A)	List Price (L)	A-L (+/−)

Summary of Required Pricing Changes and Pricing Policy Alterations

Actions:
- Inevitably the analyses will have revealed the need to modify pricing – for each product in each segment, so state the desired price.
- The stated strategy will also require changes to pricing/payment/credit policies; summarise these in the lower section of Chart P1.4.

Chart P1.5 **Summary of Distribution Requirements**

Target Market Segment:
Marketing Channel Description
Marketing Channel Changes
Stockholding/Inventory Requirements
Delivery Requirements
Transportation Issues
Overall Policy Changes:
Personnel and Service Improvements Required:
Actions: ■ State the required dealer and distribution changes necessary to facilitate target market strategy and associated marketing programmes (a) per core segment, (b) overall in the territory. ■ To facilitate the desired target market strategy, it is <u>essential</u> to have the understanding and co-operation of distributors/dealers; the recommendations on Chart P1.5 must reflect this.

Chart P1.6 Summary of Current Advertising and Promotion

Nature of Campaign
What was done, when, which promotional mix elements

Campaign Objectives
For example, create brand awareness; generate sales leads; counteract rival's campaign; support new product launch; assist dealer promotion; etc.

Cost of Programme (if known)

Results of Programme (if known)

Action:
• Complete a form per targeted segment summarising the existing promotional work being undertaken.

Chart P1.7 **Key Promotional Activity Required**

Promotional Task	Targeted Segments							
	1	2	3	4	5	6	7	8
Build brand awareness								
Build brand image								
Build product awareness								
Build product image								
Position against competitors								
Reposition against competitors								
Create primary demand for product								
Influence customers' KCVs								
Generate sales leads								
Promote after sales support								
Promote dealers/ distributors								
Support dealers' promotions								
Promote customer credit								
Influence customer buying process								
Other:								
Other:								

Actions:
- Indicate promotional requirements per targeted segment.
- Keep selections to the bare minimum - too many will not be feasible or cost effective.
- If most rows in a column are ticked, revisit the list to prioritise and to reduce the selection.

Chart P1.8 **Desired Promotional Programmes**

Target Segment:
Promotion Objectives (priorities)
Suggested Advertising and Promotions Programmes (Actual promotional tools)
Anticipated Budget Required
Timing and Scheduling of Promotional Activity
Actions: • Complete a form per targeted segment. • Ensure the recommendations reflect KCVs, desired brand positioning and the competitive position.

Chart P1.9 **Required Service Levels to Support Product Mix**

	Segment 1:	Segment 2:	Segment 3:	Segment 4:
People				
Advice/ Guidance (not consultancy)				
On-Going Support				
Facilities				
Other:				
Other:				

Any Training Requirements?

Resource/Recruitment Implications

Actions:
- This table requests information concerning service aspects of the product offer. The products *per se* (their tangible attributes) are detailed in Chart P1.3.
- Some service aspects will require retraining/orientation of personnel interfacing with customers, so state these requirements.
- These 'soft' issues connected with the product offering inevitably will require resourcing.

Chart P1.10 **Process/Customer Liaison Improvements Required**

Area Requiring Attention	Explanation/ Definition	Required Action
Market Information		
Product Information		
Flows of information for Bids/Pricing		
Demonstrations		
Handling Enquiries		
Pre-Delivery Advice (e.g. Progress Meetings)		
Commercial Support to Customers		
Technical Support		
Back-up Advice		
Payment Conditions		
Inter-personnel Relationships		
Communication With Clients		
Handling Visits		
Communication With Suppliers		
Feedback to Clients/Suppliers		
Other:		
Other:		

Actions:
- This is the business helping customers; making life easier for customers to deal with the business; improving flows of information and communications - specify such required improvements.

Chart P2.1 **Summary of Programme Tasks, Timing and Costs**

Programme Task	Person or Department Responsible	Date(s) for Activity	Anticipated Cost	Implications to the Business

Actions:
- The main marketing mix requirements from chapter P1 must be entered in column 1.
- People must now take 'ownership' of identified actions from chapter P1.

Chart P2.2 **Summary of Responsibilities**

Person or Department	Responsibility/Task	Dates/Timings

Actions:
- Allocate the tasks detailed in Chart P2.1 to individual managers or departments.
- Specify when these activities must take place.

Chart P2.3 **Summary of Costs and Budget Implications**

Task	Cost	Any Budget Implications for the Business?

Actions:
* Summarise the costs/budgets for each of the marketing programme activities detailed in chapter P1.
* Outline any implications from the combined totals of these costs.

Chart P2.4   **Summary of Likely Areas of Impacts**

Area of Impact	Implication/Required Action? By whom?

Action:
- Detail the likely knock-on impacts.

Chart P2.5 **On-Going Marketing Research Requirements**

Information Gap	Likely Research Activity	Timing	Cost

Action:
- Specify required marketing research activity.

Chart P2.6 **On-Going Work Required Summary**

Area	Required Work
Internal Structuring/ Operations	
Market Development	
Resource Base	
Products and Product Mix	
Sales Force and Customer Service	
People Issues	
Distribution and Dealers	
Promotional Activity/ Evaluation	
Pricing and Payment Terms	

Chart P2.7 **Monitoring Performance**

Monitored Issue	Expected Result (6 mths)	Actual Outcome (6 mths)	Reason for Gap	Expected Result (12 mths)	Actual Outcome (12 mths)	Reason for Gap

Actions:
- Determine measures for benchmarking progress.
- Expected results should include sales, contributions, attitudinal data relating to customers' perceptions of brand positioning (versus stated desired positioning in Chart S1.3) and their views on customer satisfaction.

Bibliography

Section I: Market Segmentation Process

Bonoma, T.V. and Shapiro, B.P. (1983) *Segmenting the Industrial Market*, Lexington, MA: Lexington Books.

Dibb, S. and Simkin, L. (1991) 'Targeting, Segments and Positioning', *International Journal of Retail and Distribution Management*, Vol. 19, No 3, pp. 4–10.

Hooley, G.J. and Saunders, J. (1993) *Competitive Positioning, the Key to Market Success*, New York, London: Prentice Hall.

Ries, A. and Trout, J. (1986) *Positioning: The Battle for Your Mind*, New York: Warner Books.

Webster, F.E. (1991) *Industrial Marketing Strategy*, New York: J. Wiley.

Wind, Y. (1978) 'Issues and Advances in Segmentation Research', *Journal of Marketing Research*, Vol. 15 (August), pp. 317–337.

Wind, Y. and Cardoza, R. (1974) 'Industrial Market Segmentation', *Industrial Marketing Management*, Vol. 3, No 2, pp. 153–166.

Yankelovich, D. (1964) 'New Criteria for Market Segmentation', *Harvard Business Review*, Vol. 42, (March–April), pp. 83–90.

Section II: Core Analyses

Analyses 1: Existing Segments/Sectors

Lockyer, K. (1983) *Production Management*, London: Pitman.

Piercy, N. (1992) *Market-led Strategic Change*, Oxford: Butterworth-Heinemann.

Wild, R. (1984) *Production and Operations Management*, Eastbourne: Holt, Rinehard and Winston.

Analyses 2: Market Trends and the Marketing Environment

Crowner, R.P. (1991) *Developing a Strategic Business Plan With Cases: An Entrepreneur's Advantage*, Homewood, IL: Irwin.

Dibb, S., Simkin, L., Pride, W. and Ferrell, O.C. (1994) *Marketing: Concepts and Strategies*, Boston: Houghton Mifflin.

Kotler, P. (1991) *Marketing Management: Analysis, Planning, Implementation and Control*, Hemel Hempstead: Prentice Hall.

Piercy, N. (1992) *Market-led Strategic Change*, Oxford: Butterworth-Heinemann.

Analyses 3: SWOT Analysis – Strengths, Weaknesses, Opportunities and Threats

McDonald, M.H. (1989) *Marketing Plans*, Oxford: Butterworth-Heinemann.

——— (1992) *The Marketing Planner*, Oxford: Butterworth-Heinemann.

Piercy, N. (1992) *Market-led Strategic Change*, Oxford: Butterworth-Heinemann.

Piercy, N. and Giles, W. (1989) 'Making SWOT Analysis Work', *Marketing Intelligence and Planning*, Vol. 7, No 5, pp. 5–7.

Weihrich, H. (1982) 'The Tows Matrix: A Tool for Situational Analysis', *Long Range Planning*, Vol. 15, No 2, pp. 54–66.

Analyses 4: Customer Needs, Expectations and Buying Processes

Assael, H. (1992) *Consumer Behavior and Marketing Action*, Boston: PWS-Kent.

Dibb, S. and Simkin, L. (1994) *The Marketing Casebook*, London: Routledge.

Ford, D. (1990) *Understanding Business Markets*, London: Academic Press.

Hutt, M.D. and Speh, T.W. (1992) *Business Marketing Management: A Strategic View of Industrial and Organizational Markets*, Fort Worth: The Dryden Press.

Piercy, N. (1992) *Market-led Strategic Change*, Oxford: Butterworth-Heinemann.

Webster, F.E. (1991) *Industrial Marketing Stretegy*, New York: J. Wiley.

Analyses 5: Competition I, The Competitive Environment

Dibb, S. and Simkin, L. (1994) *The Marketing Casebook*, London: Routledge.

Dibb, S., Simkin, L., Pride, W. and Ferrell, O.C. (1994) *Marketing: Concepts and Strategies*, Boston: Houghton Mifflin.

Doyle, P., Saunders, J. and Wong, V. (1986) 'A Comparative Study of Japanese Marketing Strategies in the British Market', *Journal of International Business Studies*, Vol. 17, No 1.

Porter, M.E. (1979) 'How Competitive Forces Shape Strategy', *Harvard Business Review*, March–April, pp. 137–145.

——— (1980) *Competitive Strategy: Techniques for Analyzing Industries and Competitors*, New York: Free Press.

——— (1985) *Competitive Advantage: Creating and Sustaining Superior Performance*, New York: Free Press.

Ries, A. and Trout, J. (1986) *Marketing Warfare*, New York: McGraw-Hill.

Saunders, J. (1991) 'Marketing and Competitive Success', in M. Baker (ed.), *The Marketing Book*, Oxford: Butterworth-Heinemann.

Sun Tzu (1981) *The Art of War*, London: Hodder and Stoughton.

Analyses 6: Competition II, Differential Advantage and Positioning

Aaker, D.A. and Shansby, J.G. (1982) 'Positioning Your Product', *Business Horizons*, May–June, pp. 56–62.

Dibb, S., Simkin, L., Pride, W. and Ferrell, O.C. (1994) *Marketing: Concepts and Strategies*, Boston: Houghton Mifflin.

Hooley, G.J. and Saunders, J. (1993) *Competitive Positioning, the Key to Market Success*, New York, London: Prentice Hall.

Ries, A. and Trout, J. (1986) *Positioning: The Battle for Your Mind*, New York: Warner Books.

Analyses 7: Assessing the Portfolio, The DPM

Hax, A.C. and Majluf, N.S. (1990) 'The Use of the Industry Attractiveness-Business Strength Matrix in Strategic Planning', in R. Dyson (ed.), *Strategic Planning: Models and Analytical Techniques*, Chichester: J. Wiley, pp. 73–92.

Hedley, B. (1977) 'Strategy and the "Business Portfolio"', *Long Range Planning*, Vol. 10, February, pp. 9–15.

McDonald, M.H. (1989) *Marketing Plans*, Oxford: Butterworth-Heinemann.

Robinson, S.J.Q., Hichens, R.E. and Wade, D.P. (1978) 'The Directional Policy Matrix – Tool for Strategic Planning', *Long Range Planning*, Vol. 11, No 3 (June), pp. 8–15.

Wensley, R. (1981) 'Strategic Marketing: Betas, Boxes, or Basics', *Journal of Marketing*, Vol. 45, Summer, pp. 173–182.

Section III: Strategy

Dibb, S., Simkin, L., Pride, W. and Ferrell, O.C. (1994) *Marketing: Concepts and Strategies*, Boston: Houghton Mifflin.

Kotler, P. (1991) *Marketing Management: Analysis, Planning, Implementation and Control*, Hemel Hempstead: Prentice Hall.

McDonald, M.H. (1989) *Marketing Plans*, Oxford: Butterworth-Heinemann.

Piercy, N. (1992) *Market-led Strategic Change*, Oxford: Butterworth-Heinemann.

Section IV: Programmes for Implementation

Programmes 1. Marketing Programmes

Crowner, R.P. (1991) *Developing a Strategic Business Plan With Cases: An Entrepreneur's Advantage*, Homewood, IL: Irwin.

Jain, S. (1993) *Marketing Planning and Strategy*, Cincinnati: South Western Publishing Company.

McDonald, M.H. (1989) *Marketing Plans*, Oxford: Butterworth-Heinemann.

Piercy, N. (1992) *Market-led Strategic Change*, Oxford: Butterworth-Heinemann.

Webster, F.E. (1991) *Industrial Marketing Strategy*, New York: J. Wiley.

Programmes 2. Resources, Schedules, Responsibilities, Implications and On-Going Requirements

Bonoma, T.V. (1985) *The Marketing Edge: Making Strategy Work*, New York: Free Press.

Kotler, P. (1991) *Marketing Management: Analysis, Planning, Implementation and Control*, Hemel Hempstead: Prentice Hall.

Piercy, N. (1989) 'Diagnosing and Solving Implementation Problems in Strategic Planning', *Journal of General Management*, Vol. 15, No 1, pp. 19–38.

——— (1990) 'Marketing Concepts and Action: Implementing Marketing-led Strategic Change', *European Journal of Marketing*, Vol. 24, No 2, pp. 24–42.

——— (1992) *Market-led Strategic Change*, Oxford: Butterworth-Heinemann.

NB: More detailed discussion on many of the concepts described in this book can be found in the following general marketing text:

Dibb, S., Simkin, L., Pride, W. and Ferrell, O.C. (1994) *Marketing: Concepts and Strategies*, Boston: Houghton Mifflin.

Index